Cover photo: Ragged and tattered after four months and 70 miles of survey, the author stands by the White River, ready to turn back.

AN OREGON BOY IN THE YUKON
A story of the Alaska Highway

Copyright © 1991 by Willis R. Grafe

Chesnimus Press
3400 Takena St., S.W.
Albany, Oregon, USA 97321

Library of Congress catalog card number 91-78007
ISBN 0-9631813-0-0 (softcover)

Printed in Canada by
D.W. Friesen and Sons
Altona, Manitoba

First edition, 1992

AN OREGON BOY
IN THE YUKON

A Story of the
Alaska Highway

To Glenn Courtney, another
builder of the society and
meeter of needs.
Read and enjoy

WILLIS R. GRAFE

Willis R Grafe

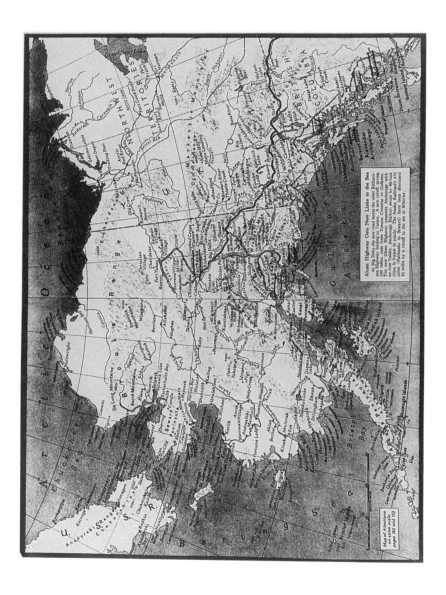

Alcan Highway Gets New Links to the Sea

At Big Delta the new road meets the older Richardson Highway leading to Valdez. A cutoff, carrying 100 miles, runs from Tanana Crossing to Gulkana. The new Glenn Highway connects Anchorage with Gulkana, and thus with Fairbanks and Valdez. Other tidewater links (to Seward, Anchorage) are at Haines. The Alaska Railroad's 470 miles (Fairbanks to Seward) have been shortened 50 miles by a cutoff to the sea at Whittier.

Map of Aleutians
See inset and
pages 152 and 153
on same scale

iv

CONTENTS

YUKON, 1943

APPENDIX

ABOUT THE AUTHOR

Growing up in rural Oregon with the NATIONAL GEOGRAPHIC as a main source of entertainment brought on an urge to see other places, even in the depths of the depression.

An English term paper on "Transportation in Alaska" was a further stimulus, and when the opportunity came to go north, the stage was set for the author to start on the story here recorded.

It doesn't end with the completion of the Alaska Highway. The whole experience was, unknowingly, to be a redirection of life goals. It all culminated in a career in the Federal Highway Administration, successor to the Public Roads Administration around which the story is built.

Completion of a B.S. and B.A. in Civil Engineering at Oregon State College in 1950 was the beginning. He then embarked on a career covering work in National Parks, National Forests and other Federal lands. To that was added responsibility for a portion of the administration of the Federal Aid program in both rural and Urban Northwest Oregon. Those were the days of the launching of the Interstate Program, the golden years of road-building.

The final seven years in Federal Service were spent in Washington D.C. as Chief of the Preliminary Engineering Branch of the Federal Projects Division, FHWA.

After all this, it was back to Oregon to the county of his birth, where he served as County Engineer for Linn County for over ten years. There it was possible to speak the language of the Feds, State, and County, all three, and encourage better vertical interagency communication.

He maintains "The best is always just over the next hill".

Introduction

There have been books and articles a plenty written about building the Alaska Highway. Even some romantic novels have sought to bring women and intrigue into the picture.

Yes, there were women there, and no doubt some intrigue, but not on a scale to make for much interest.

The short eighteen months from beginning to end of the work didn't allow much time for anything but tending to business. The Army and civilian workers who did the job were there to work and no time was available for other pursuits. They were making their contribution to winning a worldwide war, and even in isolation that goal wasn't often out of mind.

I have read whatever books I could find about building the Alaska Highway and find one thing lacking. None of the authors was there while it was going on.

What I have read primarily relates to the impact of the road on the culture, people, and land, and tells little about the road itself and how it came to be.

Unfortunately, through misunderstanding and neglect, the official records of the Public Roads Administration have been reduced to near nothing. All that remains are a dozen or so boxes of pictures in the National Archives and a few feet of shelf space in the U.S. Department of Transportation library. Much more of the fifty year old story is certainly still in the hands of participants or their families. Unfortunately, no way exists to get them all into one central location. The interest steadily wanes and soon it will be too late.

The Yukon Archives have been diligent in seeking out any information from whatever source. They are to be commended on their collection. It would be my recommendation that all records of permanent value be put into their hands for the benefit of the public.

Put down here are my recollections and observations of "How it really was". It is my hope to transfer that understanding to the mind of the reader as we share the adventure together.

Willis Grafe

TO THE YUKON

It is a constant source of wonder how small events so many times become the milestones in life. Many times they can only be identified as such by hindsight, and were not in any way planned decision points, but the culmination of a series of events not necessarily in any planned pattern.

In the face of an impending draft call, in early 1942 I was attending a training school for aircraft sheet metal assembly line workers at the old Chemawa Indian School, about five miles north of Salem.

The school was set up and operated by the National Youth Administration, and we worked alternate half days around the school to support the training and attended class the rest of the time. For the work done we received board, room, and $6.77 per month. As an outgrowth of this training I found a job as a night shift maintenance man for Columbia Aircraft Co., a small sub-assembly factory in Portland. It was located in Port of Portland Terminal No. 2, at the foot of S.E. Washington St., right at the rivers edge.

My work consisted of walking around the plant, maintaining a relatively high visibility and making any quick repairs within my capability. Higher authority and skill level was available on call, but my job was to keep the bonafide maintenance men from too many minor problems. For this I received fifty-five cents per hour, reasonable for the time.

A few weeks of this, coupled with the difficulty of getting home to my boarding house late at night when only a few of the streetcars were running, and I was ready for almost any kind of change.

To this day I don't remember just how, but I came into the knowledge that the Public Roads Administration, a branch of the Federal Works Agency, was advertising for surveyors to go to Alaska and Canada. Construction of the Alaska Highway by combined Army forces and civilian contractors was starting, and PRA was to administer the civilian engineering and construction work. I found out where the PRA was located and wandered over to see what was up.

1

The personnel office presented a bleak picture of the whole operation, including living in tent camps, etc. I suppose today this would be called "full disclosure". At any rate it sounded as if it wasn't a whole lot different than a fire camp or similar existence, and, since food was provided, I submitted an application.

The going rate for people like me, long on enthusiasm and short on knowledge, was $1,260 per year, or $105 per month, with a temporary civil service rating of SP-2, the bottom rung of the ladder. This didn't seem so bad, since they took care of food and lodging as well. I was hired on the spot by a man named Willard Scofield, and told to stand by for a call in two or three days.

I bought a small foot locker, a sleeping bag, and duffle bag, and sent all my work clothes to the laundry with a quick turnaround requested. It was quick all right. After laundry went in it was less than 24 hours before I was down begging to get it back because the train to Seattle was going out in the morning. Fortunately, the clothes were in a recoverable condition and I stuffed them and everything else I had into the trunk and bag and prepared to set out on a new adventure.

We were in Seattle two days, billeted at the Frye Hotel, while being processed through the Port of Embarkation.

Processing consisted primarily of marching in a line between two medical corpsmen who hit us with a needle in both arms at the same time. It was a rather unnerving experience for me to see the biggest and strongest appearing of all, a young man from San Francisco, faint dead away only a couple of steps away.

With the "Shots" over with we were considered ready to go.

SLOW BOAT TO SKAGWAY

We were finally called out of the Frye Hotel to go aboard our ship to Skagway. We found ourselves, each with all his gear, unloaded dockside where an old wooden steamer about 160 feet long lay in wait. Eli D. Hoyle was her name, previously unheard of by any of the passengers. I later found a painted over brass plaque with the information that she had been built in the Bellingham Shipyards in 1918, apparently part of an earlier war effort.

This proud vessel had been painted a military gray, and was part of the Army fleet more commonly known as the Army Transportation Service. We were to enjoy her appointments as a temporary troop transport. Prior to having been impressed into Army service under the emergency she had served as a cannery tender in Alaska waters.

In the superstructure there were a few cabins or staterooms and a small dining area, but our large contingent from Portland and San Francisco received blue tickets issued by the War Dept., Quartermaster Corps and labeled TROOP CLASS, our name typewritten thereon, and squadron or quarters space handwritten in as HOLD #1. This authorized us to go nine or ten feet down a ladder through the forward hatch and into a huge, gloomy room with a loose board floor above the cargo hold.

Filling the room except for the narrowest of passageways and an open area at the foot of the ladder were row after row of steel pipe bunk stanchions, three tiers high. Each of us was allowed to stake a bunk claim for the trip on a first come basis.

Burdened down with sleeping bag, leather suitcase, duffle bag, and foot locker, I made my choice of a bunk and secured it with the sleeping bag, placing the other gear around it in whatever space was available.

It was a truly motley crew which found itself preparing to share the trip. The spectrum of human variety was even exceeded by the broad range of personal equipment distributed around the dimly lit area. It ran the full range from well worn bags, trunks and sleeping gear to piles obviously quickly and recently purchased. A feeling of seeing and being part of history in the making came to me, with the "Road Rush of 42" another installment in the continuing odyssey of the Yukon. In the beginning it was only a blur of action as we prepared for the voyage ahead, but I soon began to sort out individuals from the crowd.

There were a number of regular PRA employees who were leaving home and family for an unknown period of time, but fully as many were in a category similar to mine, at least so far as time of service was concerned. Except for the family men, it was either the very young or very old, since the draft had pretty much dried up the employment pool. The urgency of the project had caused draft classification of IIB to be granted to those who might otherwise be 1A and called for military service. This would be the case until completion and return to the States.

The older men among the new hires included three or four who had followed the survey and construction business wherever it may have led, and could be called "Boomers" in the sense of the term as then used. They could be likened to the stampeders of gold rush days, with the exception that they had a little more knowledge of where they were going and what to expect than did their predecessors 45 years earlier.

There was some grumbling among the permanent PRA employees which I later learned had to do with the assignment of quarters. It seems those from the Ogden, Utah district had arrived in Seattle a day or two before the other passengers. This resulted in the early arrivals being assigned, without respect to rank or title, to the meager number of cabins aboard, plus dining room privileges. Meanwhile, relatively high ranking men from the other offices were assigned to the hold along with the rest of us troops. This situation caused some comment throughout the trip by those affected. At that time I didn't recognize or grasp the significance of this turf problem.

We cast off in the early evening, steaming our way up the sound at a steady 7 knots. Strict blackout requirements were in force, and nobody was allowed topside after dark.

Several hours into the voyage I woke to the severe pitching, rolling, and creaking of the ship, accompanied by groans of some of the less seaworthy passengers. This continued for about an hour, then subsided. I later learned the rough water occurred at the mouth of the Strait of Juan De Fuca, and was left behind as we turned north up the inside passage and into the protection of Vancouver Island. A few of the more sensitive souls had gotten seasick, but with daybreak and quieter waters they soon recovered.

The first venture to the open deck revealed us to be following a narrow waterway between wooded islands with an occasional glimpse of higher mountains behind, particularly on the starboard, or mainland side. This, with variations, was to be the view throughout the trip.

As a concession to the wartime conditions, the ship had a pair of 37mm guns mounted both fore and aft, manned by an armed guard of soldiers under command of an Army Lieutenant. This latter young man was the military commander of the ship. The crew otherwise appeared to be performing as any group of ordinary sailors, which indeed they were, having been pressed into duty along with the ship.

Those of us not privileged to use the dining room were afforded open air dining, with food dispensed out the galley door amidships as we lined up along the port rail with our steel trays. I found the food satisfactory in both quality and quantity.

For a dining table I found the large coils of hawser on the afterdeck to be the most satisfactory. Here was afforded both a nearly level place to set the tray and some shelter from the wind. At least it was, when not raining, superior to trying to negotiate the route down into the bunk area while carrying a tray full of food in one hand and clutching the ladder with the other.

So passed the time, with floating pinochle games (no gambling) and much speculation of what might be ahead.

I was not only at sea in a ship, but figuratively at sea as to what to expect so far as the job ahead was concerned. Of the manner of living, I had no qualms, particularly when listening to all the complaining regarding food, quarters, etc. from the fellow passengers. To me it was all interesting and fascinating, and promising adventure, along with $105 a month to participate. Of course those who had left families behind had reason to look at things somewhat differently.

5

It was reassuring to realize that, other than learning the job skills required, there was really nothing to be apprehensive about so far from home.

I took the occasion to seek acquaintance with the old PRA hands, and particularly enjoyed talking with Fred Johnson, an engineer from San Francisco who had done a great deal of work in the Yosemite Park area. We spent a lot of time visiting in the transverse passageway amidships where an open door allowed us to look down into the engine room. Here it was possible to enjoy the warm air rising off the old triple expansion steam engine as it labored away, carrying us ever northward at a steady seven knots.

Only one stop was made between Seattle and Skagway, not counting a wait for the tide to carry us through Wrangell Narrows. This was at Annette Island and the village of Metlakatla. It was and still is the first habitation after leaving Canadian for Alaska waters. There the Army Air Force had an airfield.

We were allowed a few hours ashore, but not before the whole contingent of passengers was mustered on the dock and given a lecture on shore leave conduct. A young Lieutenant provided us with what must have been the standard lecture for a shipload of troops, cautioning us not to do evil to the town or its citizens, act responsibly, and be sure to return as scheduled. Some quizzical looks were passed around the group, as if to say "What kind of a bunch of guys does he think he's talking to?" or some other perhaps less reserved opinion.

Prior to our departure from the dock, the stevedores had opened the after hatch and begun unloading bombs. This had a sobering effect on the group, but not enough to inhibit their visit ashore. We later learned that in our forward hold, our beds were riding atop similar cargo, to be unloaded on the return trip. I suppose in these more cautious days smoking would have been restricted in our bunkroom.

There wasn't much at Metlakatla, but it was a welcome chance to go ashore and take a walk through the Indian village.

Here we saw our first muskeg swamps as we walked the wooden walkways beside the road. It is similar to the permafrost we would encounter in future work, yet different

6

in that these swamps were deeper with no hard underlying frozen soil.

Although the shore of the channel as we went further north was a continuation of what had gone before, it became more and more impressive, possibly because it was closer to us as the waterway narrowed. At any rate it seemed the mountains got higher and closer and the clouds lower, and there was no denying the weather got colder and wetter. This to a degree discouraged sightseeing and kept us more and more confined to our narrow bunks in the burrow beneath the deck.

WAR DEPARTMENT
QUARTERMASTER CORPS
Form 160-C
Approved Jan. 27, 1937

UNITED STATES ARMY TRANSPORT

TROOP CLASS

Name   *Squadroom*

GRAFE, W. R., EMP., PRA

3—10632

Waiting for the train Gillenwater, Bassett, Trudgeon, Strawn, Grafe.

Main Street, Skagway

SKAGWAY-PULLEN HOUSE

We finally docked at Skagway, only to find no provision had been made for quarters. Just like the earlier stampeders, we were on our own in a town already overtaxed by the first contingent of Army troops. In 1942 Skagway had not expanded its facilities since about 1900, the end of the gold rush. The old wood frame hotels with names like "Golden North" and "Pack Trail Inn" were still the backbone of the downtown area.

Far at the north edge of town was the Pullen house, operated by Mrs. Harriet Pullen and her granddaughter. There five of us decided to go, leaving our major pile of baggage in the tender care of the railroad freight handlers. It was over a quarter of a mile away so we didn't really have much choice. I had read of Mrs. Pullen, a highly respected widow lady dating from the gold rush days, and how she had supported her two sons there in those frantic times. She had remained afterward to become a pillar of the community and a legend in her own time.

We were able to get rooms in the hotel by virtue of being faster walkers than some others, and after getting settled, wandered back downtown in search of food. No advance travel funds had been provided or any arrangements made for meals, so we were on a rather austere budget.

Meal prices were a traumatic discovery, so Bill Gillenwater, a camp cook, suggested we go grocery shopping instead and eat back at the hotel. Having no real alternative made the decision an easy one, and we quickly concurred.

As a result, the boys from Oregon, Billie Bassett, Ken Strawn, Bill Gillenwater, Roy Trudgeon, and I came back to the hotel and wandered into the lobby carrying our groceries, not without some apprehension.

There sat Mrs. Pullen, a statuesque lady of seventy some years, presiding over the establishment like the queen she truly was. Spotting the grocery bags, she smiled and said "Good evening boys".

We responded in kind with a "Good evening". By this time it must have been 9 PM, although still daylight.

9

"What's new this evening?" she inquired.

Bill, being the senior member, meekly described our plans for dinner.

Another smile from our benevolent hostess, then "You've no need to eat in your rooms, you know, just bring your things into the kitchen and join us while we visit. I want to hear about all this frantic activity which surrounds us."

Much relieved, we gladly accepted the invitation and followed her into the spacious kitchen. There Bill put together the results of our shopping trip into a meal as we sat around the table with her.

Truly, this was a gracious lady and it was an experience not to be forgotten.

Bennett Station

OVER THE HILL TO WHITEHORSE

After one night in Skagway we reported to the train station at the foot of Main Street, where we were put aboard the White Pass and Yukon Railroad train to Whitehorse. At that time it was still on a normal schedule, having not yet been impacted by the war effort.

I am reasonably sure the coaches were some of the original rolling stock, put in place before 1900 when the road first went into operation. In any case, they were classic narrow-gauge wooden bodied cars with the traditional pot-bellied coal stove in each end and wicker seats, reversible by swinging the back to face the preferred direction.

Steam was the motive power, and four engines were spaced throughout the train to take us for the first thirty or so miles of the trip, up the river and over White Pass to the stop at Bennett Station. At that point the extra engines were removed and a single puffer billy took the cars for the next 80 miles. This last was all downhill, since we had crossed over into the Yukon drainage.

Snow was six or eight feet deep at the pass, up to the eaves of the buildings, but as we went a few miles further to Bennett it decreased to only a light cover.

The train carried no dining cars, but stopped at Bennett for lunch while the train crew removed the extra engines.

There were probably 100 passengers on the train, including a detachment of soldiers, all of whom must be fed a quick lunch, and it appeared the establishment was somewhat overtaxed and overwhelmed by the crowd.

When we filed in to sit down, what appeared to be dessert in the form of apple pie, cheese, and sweet pickles was already in place on the long tables. After waiting in our seats for a time, we came to realize our lunch was already in front of us. Accordingly, we stocked up on pie, cheese, and pickles, which were in abundance, with plenty of resupply. I like pie, or anything else edible for that matter, so was content, but there was some grumbling among the more conventional eaters.

Back aboard the now shortened train for the final run

11

along Lake Bennett and to the village of Carcross. There we stopped for perhaps 45 minutes while the soldiers formed up into marching units and exercised up and down the railroad yard in the cold wind.

On to Whitehorse, where we arrived in the late afternoon. Here, in contrast to Skagway, our quarters had already been arranged for in one of the three hotels, the White Pass, Regina, or Whitehorse Inn.

I was booked into the White Pass, to share a room and bed with Avery Wheelwright, a permanent employee from Utah. Our window faced out upon the freight depot. The whole river front was a scene of activity. Here the rails and river boats met, and all freight downriver had to be transferred from land to water. The river had only a couple of weeks before lost its cover of ice, and the big river boats had already been launched from their winter drydock and brought alongside the dock behind the rail station for loading. What a fascinating sight.

Whitehorse Rapids and Miles Canyon just upriver from town constituted a barrier to navigation for the big boats, although once above them it was possible to navigate much further. During the gold rush the canyon and rapids had been navigated only downstream by rafts built at Lake Bennett.

Near White Pass

POINTS NORTH AND WEST

After a few days of freight handling and other busy work, we were assigned to a field survey crew and prepared to head into the bush to begin the work we came for.

I had been assigned to a survey crew led by Fred Johnson, my friend of the boat trip. We were to do a preliminary location survey for the route of the highway beginning 150 or 200 miles northwest of Whitehorse at Burwash Landing on Kluane Lake and proceeding northwest to a crossing of the White River.

Other parties had been assigned to adjacent sections. So far as I know, ours was the longest continuous section assigned to a single party in the whole 1500 miles of the highway.

Fifteen of us were assigned originally and told to leave all excess personal gear in storage, taking only a bedroll, duffel bag and one piece of hand baggage. This was easy for me, since my foot locker could keep all the rest. Actually, I took only a duffel bag and sleeping bag, leaving the rest in a vacant church building which had been rented by the PRA as a storehouse.

There was great variety in the personnel of the crew. Only Fred, his assistant Lowell Jensen from Utah, and Harry French and J.H. Tucker were career employees. In addition, the two mail room employees from San Francisco, Archie Erickson and Clyde Hill made up the last of those with previous PRA ties. All the rest of us were new hires. That isn't to say it was a totally inexperienced group. Our Transitman, Bill Ash, had been with Los Angeles County several years, and, although new to the organization, had a wealth of experience. Ken Strawn, with only one term to go at Oregon State to graduate in Civil Engineering, also possessed good experience and training.

Hugh Kelly from Eureka, Ca., was the son of County Surveyor and had learned well at his fathers' knee.

Billie Bassett had worked on logging railroad survey and construction for some time for the Oregon American Lumber Co., at Vernonia, Ore., and also for Weyerhaeuser Co.

13

Home in Whitehorse

1st Ave., Whitehorse

Yukon River Steamer "Casca" — White Pass and Yukon Route

Shipyard

And then there were the rest, all prepared with enthusiasm and good health to offer and a great variety of unrelated experience. Archie and Clyde with their mail room experience were primarily qualified because they were already on board when the call came. They did not volunteer, they were sent. Jack Edwards had been a collection agent for a finance company in San Francisco. Tom Kirkwood, a Canadian prospector in his late twenties was hired locally as an axeman and was a valuable asset in many practical ways.

Last, as for me, I guess my visiting with Fred had caused him to select me, since at least he identified me as more than just a name on the list.

There were those of Fred's peers who prophesied doom for him in taking out such a motley crew, but I like to believe he was looking beyond experience to attitude and enthusiasm, and time proved his judgment to be sound.

Our trip to Burwash Landing was to be made in sections, since the old Curtis Condor biplane of the Yukon Southern Air Transport had a limited capacity, both for bulk and weight.

From the airport on the hill above Whitehorse we took off for the northwest over a land of ice-bordered rivers and frozen lakes. The coastal mountains on our left loomed white and mysterious clear to the horizon.

The two hour 150-mile flight was a real transition from the town to the landing on frozen Kluane Lake, where the ice was still four feet thick and solid.

We quickly off-loaded our gear and struggled ashore and up the bank to our assigned quarters. For me it was a one room cabin for six, quickly dubbed the "Boars Nest". This was to be home for the next few weeks while we started our survey and completed all that was within reasonable walking distance. (About five miles in each direction)

BURWASH LANDING

The coming of the survey crew and the promise of changes to come could not help but have had an impact far greater than we could comprehend at the time.

The trading post at Burwash landing had been established in the early 1900's by Gene and Louis Jacquot, two young frenchmen who, as I understood at the time, were in flight from conscription into the armed forces. The post was situated on the south bank of Kluane Lake at the far northwestern end. At the opposite end was the village of Kluane, or Silver City. Supplies were brought in from Whitehorse once or twice a year by truck to Silver city, about 150 miles over a primitive road, then transported 40 miles down the lake by boat and barge to Burwash. Silver City had at one time been a busy staging area for the gold rush in the area. In contrast, Burwash had always been primarily a trading post providing for the needs of the native population and itinerant trappers and prospectors. Some provisioning for hunting parties had also become a major factor in later years.

The post had developed the self-sufficiency typical to such locations. It included a blacksmith shop, small steam sawmill, greenhouse, a large barn, and other subsidiary buildings. The actual trading was carried on in a store building containing clothing, prospecting and camping supplies, staple groceries, and other necessities.

Several locally built boats were pulled up high on the shore when we arrived, waiting breakup of the lake ice.

The trader maintained a large garden across the lake on the warmer north shore, thus providing vegetables appropriate to the climate.

About a quarter of a mile east up the lake was a native village, consisting of a dozen or so cabins with a population of about 40 Athapaskans.

In the summer months there were always dogs in evidence, but they were tied when not working. Much of the time there was a symphony of barking, only stopped by a sharp reprimand.

17

Kloo Lake, Burwash Bound

Yukon Southern Air Transport, Curtis Condor, Burwash Ldg.

Burwash Landing

Boar's Nest

Our fifteen man crew included two Canadian axemen, and we were housed in three of the cabins. Besides the six of us in the Boars Nest, six more were in another down by the lake shore and Chief Fred, Lowell Jensen, and Ken Strawn bunked in the office about 50 yards to the south.

Arrangements had been made for us to eat at the dining room where Gene and his wife Pete did the cooking, assisted by Babe and Belle Dickson,(Pete's sisters) and Ada Watt, a native girl of about 16 years. Pete, Belle, and Babe were half native, daughters of Tom Dickson, a retired RCMP trooper, who at that time was very old and nearly blind.

Both Gene and Louis Jacquot were at that time well over sixty, Louis somewhat the older, probably near 70.

The food was adequate by my standards, although some complained. The garden provided plenty of potatoes and the primary source of meat was corned moose, preserved in brine like fresh corned beef. Ham was the only imported meat, no beef at all while we were there. The greatest lack I felt was fresh milk, which was true throughout my time in the north. I just never could learn to appreciate canned milk except for cooking.

Our lunches were made up individually from supplies laid out, mostly ham sandwiches and dried fruit. No canned goods at all was available, primarily due to high cost and difficulty of shipment.

The ham was not as currently experienced, but was real old country ham, smoked and very salty. We were from time to time concerned about the green sheen which occasionally showed on the lunch slices but comforted ourselves by always building a lunch fire and thoroughly cooking it before eating.

Pan American Airways, who pioneered commercial air service to Alaska, maintained a radio station at Burwash, manned by Hughie Stone and Gordon Warren. They kept a 24 hour watch and standby schedule. Pan Am had built and maintained the largest building at the landing, a two story log lodge about 30 by 48 feet, designed and equipped to provide for whatever emergency might occur. The only time I ever saw it used was when Gene utilized the big range to roast a swan for our Sunday dinner.

The airstrip was situated about a mile away from the

20

landing by way of a poor and rutted road, usable by vehicles only if frozen or dry. A severe crosswind was characteristic of the strip, so most aircraft used the lake ice whenever it was sound.

Our first day of work was the day after arrival, no time lost here. After breakfast and lunch preparation we started up the lake to the southeast, directly into the teeth of a strong and biting wind. This went on for about two hours, after which we went ashore, up the bank and inland for about a quarter of a mile to a relatively flat, open area among the small spruce and cottonwood trees. Here Chief Fred said, "this is where we start, Engineers station nought plus nought nought. (0+00). This meant we started at that point, measuring in one hundred foot stations and placing and measuring angle points in the line to establish field data from which to design a highway.

This historic moment was observed by driving a short wooden "hub" into the frozen ground and placing a tack in the center, over which to hang the plumb bob of the transit. This assured proper location of the instrument to turn the angle between the rear and forward courses on the line. In this case, however, there was no backsight to refer to, so a compass bearing was used, later to be corrected by use of a polar observation (North Star shot). At this latitude, 63 degrees north, a polar observation is difficult because of the elevation of the north star and difficulty of observation. Furthermore, the magnetic compass bearings are also somewhat less than reliable.

At last I was beginning to learn about surveying, the first lesson being that a hub was not always the middle of a wheel, but may be a stick in the ground with a tack in it. After that day a lot of terms which had previously been mysterious and obscure began to make sense.

Early on it seemed to me most of the work of surveying was cutting brush for the more skilled and experienced to come along behind, measuring distances and angles. Of course, if they can't see, they can't survey. We did have two local men hired to be axemen, but any extra help from the rest of the crew was welcome. Because I could chop either right or left handed, I sometimes got opportunities to work harder on the bigger trees.

After the first two days of apprenticeship I was assigned to the "topog" crew, which comes along last in the procession, measuring distance and elevation changes right and left of the line to enable the plotting of a contour map from the data. Bill Bassett, another Oregonian, and I did this under supervision and were always catching up with everybody else and being rewarded with the opportunity to cut brush. We hadn't yet learned that a days work didn't necessarily mean you went full speed all day. It seemed the more experienced hands were able to keep busy with their surveying and avoid chopping brush more successfully than we did.

The work day was short and the walking long, and we traveled one way on our own time, the other on pay. It was in total a long day, growing shorter as we worked toward camp and longer as we were going away from camp.

Progress averaged about a mile a day, but largely depended on terrain and ground cover. Again, the brush cutting was controlling much of the time. In this way it took about ten working days for us to reach the outer walking limits from five miles south to five miles north of Burwash. It then became necessary to move out into tent camps.

We were able to walk on the lake ice for over a week, never troubled by fighting brush or walking our survey line to work all that time. A primitive road as far as the Duke River, about four miles to the northwest was also a great help.

Not so fortunate with the ice was Bob Reeve, an Alaska bush pilot who was doing some flying for the Army. About the second week we were at the landing he brought in a party of engineers involved with the railroad reconnaissance and landed at the airstrip. Since the mile walk to the post was too far for his taste, he decided to take the plane over to the lake and land on the ice. This he did, coming down on the marked out strip between the rows of little trees lying on the ice. The landing was fine, but when he started to taxi toward shore the honeycombed and mushy afternoon spring ice failed him and started to yield beneath his wheels. He immediately cut the engine, just as the left wheel went through. The other was right behind, and there was Bob, sitting helpless inside NC7034, which was lying belly down on the ice. Several of us had been watching from shore, un-

22

able to do anything, since the ice had melted back from the shore during the late afternoon.

Bob got out of the plane, retrieved his personal gear and logbook and walked toward shore on the treacherous ice. We laid out a long plank across the shoreline moat and he tiptoed ashore.

Right then things looked pretty bleak for him and his party.

Next morning the lake ice had pretty well refrozen and was safe for a few hours to launch a rescue operation.

Begrudgingly Fred decided it would be all right if we delayed going to work until we had rendered all the rescue assistance at our disposal.

Gene Jacquot provided some large timbers which we laid across beneath the engine to prevent any further settlement. Then a tripod was constructed above the engine hub to support a set of half-ton chainblocks, not enough to lift the plane. Again, a rigid platform was build beneath the engine hub to support a hydraulic jack. The sequence adopted was to jack up the hub, take up the slack with the chain blocks, raise the jack, and then repeat the operation. In a matter of a couple of hours, well before the ice became mushy, we had the wheels up and on planks. The propeller had been only slightly bent at the tips, and Gene was able to quickly straighten it out in the blacksmith shop. Bob took off before the ice got too soft, moving the plane over to the airstrip to be parked until further action was taken to assure airworthiness. The survey crew went off to work and Bob called for another plane to come rescue him and his party.

The book *Glacier Pilot* by Beth Day, the story of Bob Reeve, gives his version of this episode beginning on page 175. It is somewhat different than here related because of his perception that a hundred or more construction workers were responsible for his plight. For the record it must be pointed out that in May, 1942 construction had not yet started and the Army wasn't within a hundred miles of Burwash Landing. The decision to try the ice was his alone, and all we did was to help him out of a bad situation. He said at the time if any of us ever ran across him in again, to identify ourselves, and the dinner would be on him. I came close a few times, but never quite made it.

Kluane Lake Shore

First Survey Point O+OO, Vuckovich, F. Johnson, Tucker, French, Ash, Edwards

SOCIAL LIFE AT BURWASH

Although the morning walks up the lake facing the wind, the active surveying or brush cutting all day, and the long walks home should have been enough to weary the body, the long northern daylight still stimulated a certain amount of evening activity. Like most western societies though, it was Saturday night which became the bright spot for the few weeks we were at Burwash Landing.

The Pan Am radio operators had among their possessions what in Canada is called a "Gramophone", (Phonograph to us) and a meager collection of records which were made available to the local younger set, Babe, Belle, and Ada, our dining room help.

The dining room, about 12 by 24 feet, would be cleared for action, and the linoleum floor swept clean for the weekly "Burwash Bounce". The bouncers were our young single crewmen, whichever radio operator was off shift, and the three girls. All the records were fast, and I was given to understand the step used was the "one step". Only portions of one tune remain in my memory, and only one title, *The Dance of the Roses*. The melody as I recall is here included and the words ended with the plea "I'm sorry that's all I can say". The dancing would go on until one or two AM or until all gave up in exhaustion, especially the girls, who, being outnumbered, were much in demand. Occasionally younger girls would come from the Native village to sit and watch, but they were too shy to participate.

DANCE OF THE ROSES

Other recreational aspects of the area were outdoor oriented, with fishing the favorite of some, but the prospect of a hike and fishing trip after working on the line all week wasn't too appealing.

All but the Oregon boys seemed to have an aversion to

25

rain, so when the first good storm came, Fred decided to give the troops the day off to rest. It was a welcome time to wash clothes, rest, write, read, or for other rehabilitative activity, but not so for the fishermen. Three of them took advantage of the time off to go a couple of miles down the lake to a small stream and try their luck. Unfortunately for the rest of the workers, when Fred heard about it his reaction was typical and positive. "What's the matter with these guys, they think they can't work in the rain, then go fishing and get wet anyway?". That was the first and last time there was any time off for wet weather, and probably rightly so.

The lake ice lasted only long enough to let us finish our work south of the landing, at which point the lake surface was no longer needed as a route to work. The breakup was to me spectacular. A strong southeast wind came up, breaking the ice as it swept down the lake. It was blown to the northwest end, where it stacked up in huge piles like land borne icebergs.

Although we continued to work out of Burwash until the walk became far too long for any efficiency, the failure of our camp equipment to arrive forced it, since we couldn't establish a camp.

As a final effort to continue work from there, we built a footbridge across the Duke river, a glacial stream about four miles to the west. It consisted of two poles lashed to log piers in the river, all placed by the use of handlines and muscle power in the cold, rushing water. The bridge managed to survive for a little over a week, long enough for us to get so far away with the work that the days weren't long enough to accomplish much after walking to the end of the line and back.

CAMP ON BURWASH CREEK

Finally the camp equipment began to arrive via float plane, and the word was passed that our days at Burwash Landing were soon to end. With the first plane came the first mail, about a month from the time we had sailed from Seattle. Money also came in the mail, and none to son, since it was necessary to make a few purchases prior to moving to camp.

The supplies and mail shifted the emphasis for a while from social activities to letter writing, laundry, and similar activities in anticipation of a long spell of isolation.

When four planeloads of supplies and a cook (but no stove) had arrived, orders came to have our gear packed and stacked, ready for movement to the new campsite eleven miles northwest.

After all day on the line, the crew arrived at the new campsite to find it unoccupied, so, after cutting a supply of poles and wood, we sat down in the mosquito filled fresh air to await whatever was going to happen. Then came the rain, and three of us had just completed building a shelter when the packtrain of about a dozen horses arrived. This first load contained bedrolls, tents, a little food, and not much else. Despite the usual first time blues, the cook managed to get some dinner over an open fire, and enough tents were set up for shelter by about 9 PM that we could bed down for our first night in camp.

Meanwhile, back at Burwash the packers had also been experiencing first day blues with the horses.

Each spring the horses are rounded up from the open river bars where they have roamed freely all winter and have, over the eight months of idleness developed a resistant and rebellious spirit. This bodes evil for the unfortunate wrangler or packer who must break them to pack all over again each spring. Our move was no exception. The efforts of Jimmie Joe and Sam Johnson, our permanent Indian packers, along with, I guess, any other available able bodied people at Burwash, were necessary to just get the first small consignment loaded out in time for us to have a little food and

Bob Reeve, Down on his luck Reeve, Kelly, Edwards, S. Johnson, Gene Jacquot, Jensen

Ada Watt and Jean Jacquot

Sam roasts a rib

Packing horses on the Donjek Sam Johnson, Louis Jacquot, Tom Kirkwood

shelter for the night. Subsequent trips improved, but not much.

On day two the pack string came in about 3 PM, still without a cook stove, to the consternation of the cook, Ray Hinton. He nevertheless kept us adequately fed by use of the open fire. Things began to get a little strained after the first 24 hours, though, and the psychological need for a cook-stove became more acute with every passing hour.

The first full day after moving into camp was spent getting used to the new life and learning how to set up camp for maximum convenience during the estimated ten to four-teen day stay there.

The cook tent, 16x20 feet and about thirteen feet high at the gable, required all hands to erect, but, despite the lack of a stove to use it, was soon erected. A log frame was con-structed to hold the table and a log supported by posts driven into the ground formed a bench on each side. The table top consisted of narrow slats about three feet long spaced slightly apart and encased in a canvas cover. This enabled the whole dining table, normally about three by twelve feet, to be rolled up into a cylinder about 18" in diameter and three feet long, the width of the table. All that was necessary to have a din-ing table was to drive three or four stakes into the ground in two rows, lay a small pole along their tops reasonably level, and the call came to "Roll out the table". Not exactly as stimulating an activity as referred to in the famous polka, but at least the meter was correct and it always marked a mile-stone in the setting up of camp.

Utensil racks, pot and pan racks, storage, etc., consisted of a combination of poles and nails. Having everything ac-cessible and visible was the first requirement. Storage was easily solved by use of the packing cartons for food and the pack boxes for everything else.

Contrary to current belief, refrigeration is not mandato-ry for survival. When the only perishable foods are as durable as eggs and bacon, life is relatively simple. Initially we were supplied with a side of fresh beef, but after that was gone we were on our own. with authority to harvest game for camp use.

Bunk tents were ten by twelve feet, with four men each except for the office tent, which held two men plus equipment for the office. In the center of each tent was a "Sibley" heating stove, a cone shaped creature of sheet metal with the stovepipe mounted atop the peak, pointing straight up. A door on the side provided access to the firebox. No bottom was attached, so it sat on the dirt floor of the tent, requiring some creativity on the part of the occupants to provide some draft control. Clever use of cans from the kitchen enabled the fire to be adequately controlled, with draft designs improving as the season progressed. The practicality of these stoves was well demonstrated when they were nested and mounted crosswise stop the packs, only needing to be fastened by a rope running up through the bottom of the stove and threaded through the pipe hole. This would work well so long as the rope remained tightly secured to the pack, but a little slack caused a lot of noise and movement and the whole rattly thing could spook a horse. A faster gait then compounded the problem until some sort of disaster ultimately occurred. The constant flexing of the unsupported metal cone made it difficult to keep the tiedown secure, and the tree limbs and branches along the way would add to the problem.

I could hardly believe my eyes when I saw the horses come in loaded with folding canvas cots and cotton mattresses. Way back in Portland, what seemed like years before, really only about a month, I had been painted a work picture of genuine hardship, but here we were in wall tents and sleeping up off the ground. The wisdom of this was soon apparent when four men sought to store all their personal possessions in the tent. The storage under the bed was all there was, and without it things would have been unbearably crowded. As it was, with a place to sit and storage as well, it was fairly comfortable.

The cookstove finally arrived at the landing on the fifth and last planeload. There it was, a big, 200 pound cast iron beauty. Sight of it prompted a quick confrontation between Gene Jacquot and Fred. "Not on one of my horses, you don't" said Gene, and the battle was joined, or so the incident was reported to us.

There was a lot at stake for Fred. A hungry and waiting crew, an anguished cook, and the whole Alaska-Canada war effort hanging in the balance. The upshot of it was that a horse came into our camp carrying not one, but two stoves. Light, boxy sheet metal ones with a small oven and even smaller firebox each, and so the day was saved and maybe the war. These stoves had been good enough for Gene's hunting camps, why not for us? Four stakes driven into the ground to support them and the cook was in business. Negotiations for the relative values of the stoves would wait for a later time. Thus the stage was finally set for the next two weeks at Burwash Creek camp and the season ahead.

On this first move from the landing to Burwash Creek I helped the packers unload and saddle up for the morning return trip, and got to know them a bit. I had done a little work with horses on fire crews and was able to impress them with my meager skills. As a result, all during the future camp moves at Jimmie Joe's request, I was first to come off the survey and give them help. This suited me fine, since it allowed some variety and the opportunity to get to know more about the country. I enjoyed working with them and learned a lot about horses.

Each day the mosquitoes were worse, with no relief except as the nights would cool down and they would tire like the rest of us. The myth of a smudge of smoke intimidating them was found to be just that, a myth. Dinner was an effort with the bugs all over the food and the smudge fire of green spruce boughs making the eyes burn and water. The repellant of those days came in a green bottle labelled "Sta-Away" and was only slightly effective for a short time. The only reasonable remedy when at work was to wear two thicknesses of clothing and head nets. That way each time you moved you body it would clinch their beaks and the face was screened off. My old Army campaign hat with its broad brim was ideal for the headnet, giving me plenty of breathing room. Billie Bassett carefully stitched a small, cigarette-sized hole in his net so he could smoke while still under protection.

Burwash Creek, site of our camp, was a well known gold bearing area and much of the creek had long been claimed, probably not long after the gold rush of 1898, 44 years earlier.

Our camp was situated on a claim belonging to Paul Burkett, who lived at Burwash, but nobody ever knew him to work it. Upstream from us, however, lived Zeke, busily scratching out an existence on a claim and exciting our imagination.

One evening after work, Jack Edwards, Bill Bassett, and I decided to make a call on him, since there still remained plenty of daylight. It was necessary to wade the creek several times on this journey, and Bill and I went ahead, not realizing Jack was no longer following close behind. We never did find Zeke, and had given up and turned back down the creek, when, over on the other side we spotted Jack, busily engaged in building a shelter for the night. At last he saw us, whereupon he lifted one foot and pointed to the bottom of his moccasins, where, even from that distance, we could plainly see his bare toes.

Not realizing moosehide moccasins are made for cold, dry weather, not wading, he had done irreparable damage to them and started in on his tender feet.

We sympathized with him and walked on back to camp and turned in. After a bit Bill's compassion got the best of him and he got up about 11:30 and carried Jack's boots up to him so he could walk back to camp.

Boot Greasing time, Hard Luck Creek. Strawn, Bassett, Grafe, Edwards, Erickson

33

Crossing the Donjek

Pickhandle Lake. Fred says "Take him back" Replacement, Pilot
Harvey, Fred J. Harry French

CAMP LIFE IS DIFFERENT

Moving from Burwash Landing had both pluses and minuses. On the plus side, once we were set up, was a change to food more like what we were used to. Ray Hinton, our cook, was, like many camp cooks, something of a prima donna, but he spared no effort or resource to provide good and adequate food. During those wartime years in the States severe rationing was in force. Not so for us, our effort had been given top priority and no departure from normal camp diet was evident. The dried fruit at the landing was replaced with canned goods of nearly any variety, and in the beginning we were even supplied with fresh beef, all brought in on the horses. The first shipment of beef was the last, however, and after a few weeks the packers shot our first moose.

The little lightweight stoves were reasonably satisfactory, and a plentiful supply of baked goods was always on hand. For me, except for the lack of fresh milk, it was the most sumptuous table I had ever experienced. We couldn't afford it at home, and certainly Oregon State College or the Chemawa Indian School couldn't compare, despite their more sophisticated cooking facilities. The diet was a real change for our packers Jimmie Joe, Sam Johnson, and little Louis Jacquot. Canned fruit and vegetables as well as occasional fresh oranges and apples were not a part of their world.

There were minor minuses or drawbacks to being in camp rather than where the social life was more stimulating, but for the most part we were so busy working and surviving that it wasn't noticed.

Under wartime rules we worked a six day week, which was not a burden, since there wasn't much else to do but take care of personal needs in the off time. Every Sunday was busy doing just that, with laundry being the biggest time user. Mobilizing the hot water, tubs, soap and washboard took time, and competition for the use of the equipment was often keen.

The mountain peaks along the south side of the valley were about 6600 feet in elevation, four thousand feet above us and, even after walking all week, on more than one occasion a climb was made. The glaciers on these mountains fed several tumbling streams, all of which showed some evidence of past gold prospecting. The lure of gold was a good motivator, and almost every week one or more of the crew would try a little prospecting. The cracks in the bedrock of the streams were always the best, having acted as a natural sluicebox over the years. It was nearly always possible to get a little color in the pan to keep the interest up.

Standards of bodily cleanliness vary with people, and our crew was no exception. The sheer difficulty of heating the water in a five gallon can over the open fire and crouching down in the washtub in the mosquito infested air was enough to make a bather give thoughtful consideration before committing himself to more than a minimum amount of purity.

About six weeks into the camp routine, when vulnerability to the supply system began to be felt. First it was the lack of fresh meat. In cleaning up the moose meat, some of it had been washed rather than allowed to crust over and be trimmed, resulting in spoilage which we could ill afford. Our packers, wise in such matters, had not spoken up when they saw the meat being soaked in water, rather let the boss and others learn without them having to be the teachers. Nevermore was water applied to fresh meat.

Fortunately, at this, our first time of need, a reconnaissance team of the 29th Engineers, led by Lieut. Firmin and Sgt. Bill Croft, came by at a convenient time and left us a large piece of caribou, good for a few days.

By mid June we were harvesting Dall sheep from the hills above camp.

As the season wore on, shortages of one kind or another occurred, but the supply system really only came apart one time, when between June 19 and Aug 6 we had no resupply to supplement our sheep and moose. To make it worse, on July 13 all the non-Canadians were required to turn in their guns for registration, leaving only our Canadian Axeman, Tom Kirkwood and his .30-.30 carbine for hunting. The first time out with it alone he and Ken Strawn cleanly missed two sheep at short range. When I sighted it in on a target in the lake that night it was shooting about four feet to the

36

left in about 60 yards. Plenty bad enough to miss a sheep. Hunting success improved after appropriate adjustment to the sights.

My letter of August 14 to my brother Herman gives a much more detailed description of the problem and efforts at solution, and is included.

Starvation Camp
Hard Luck Creek
August 14, 1942

Dear Dad and Herman

I got your letters of July 23, 28, and 30 on Aug. 8. It seems there is a delay somewhere, perhaps because we haven't had any mail at all in since July 9, what do you think?

Since that last bit of information I wrote, a lot of things have happened in the dear old PRA camp.

Our supply plane which was supposed to land on August 1 failed to show itself over camp, so our chief, Fred Johnson, took off down the valley thirty miles to a large lake where he made an attempt to flag one down with a big smoke, which he didn't succeed in doing. We ran out of butter, bacon, sugar, flour, eggs, and other things too numerous to mention. While he was gone, ten days, he ran out of everything but salt and tea and had to shoot a moose to keep from starving.

We who remained in camp were in a sad way. Two of the boys went up on the hill above camp to hunt sheep and shot 18 times and left one dead over a cliff where they couldn't get at it. The next morning two of the fellows and I left at 4 A.M. and went up after one. We got to the top about 7:30, just before they were starting to feed. They were all lying on the west side in the cliffs, still in the shade. One of the fellows shot a small one which turned all four feet in the air and fell. We all rushed up to the top of the hill to take pictures before they all got away and I think I got some good ones. I'll send you some when I get them. When we got done taking pictures, we went back down the hill to dress out our sheep and take him down off the mountain. When we got there, we found blood all over the rocks and a few bone slivers as well, but no sheep. One of the boys thought he had seen it running away, and we really figured we were skunked, so sat down to eat lunch and think it over. We decided to go down the other side of the mountain after the ones we had spooked, a band of about fifty lambs and ewes and ten or twelve rams. We went down over the hill and couldn't find a single sheep anywhere, so resigned ourselves to our bad luck and went back to take another look for the original victim. One of the fellows and I went down over the cliffs, and the other took our equipment around and down below. We started down the face of the cliffs and came to a place where we were not very sure of safe navigation. I started around the face and got to where I was hung on the side and couldn't move either way and was spreadeagled flat against it. I finally kicked loose a rock and got a foothold where I could jump by pivoting out over the cliff edge with my rear foot and hoping to land on a loose rock slide. I got through all right, but the other fellow, being shorter, couldn't follow me and went back up, around, and down after our partner to the bottom of the cliff. I worked my way on down the slide and finally found the sheep on a rock ledge about 20 yards down. I dragged, kicked, and rolled him on down the hill to where it would be possible to get to him from below. The others came around the hill to where I was and we dressed it out and brought it down to camp. It lasted only about three or four meals and again we were out of meat. Three days later two of the boys went back up on the hill and not a sheep was in sight, but they could see them with glasses on another hill a couple of miles away. They went over after them, but shot and missed, and the sheep all ran away. They really felt low when they came back to camp. The man who had shot the other one and I went early the next morning and sat up on the hill for about an hour waiting for sheep and nearly froze. Finally we located three on a hill about a mile and a half away, so went over after them. We still hunted for about half an hour and finally shot one which took a header over a thirty foot cliff and rolled about 100 more down before it finally stopped. When I got down to it I found its back was broken clear in two from the shot and all that had held it from going over the cliffs was the intestines which had come out through the back and hung up on a rock about thirty feet up the hill. I took it back to the top of the hill and we dressed it out and tied it onto our packboards. I imagine it weighed about 120 pounds. I had the front quarters and rib cage and he the hind quarters, gun, liver and heart. We carried it down for about five miles. We had plenty of meat for a while and a few fish from the creek running through camp.

On Aug. 7, an Army Lieutenant and his aide came through camp and left us sugar enough for a couple of days. On the evening of Aug. 8, a plane flew over a lake about two miles above camp, left for about an hour, and then came back, landed, and took off again. Two of the crew went up to see what was going on and found a load of food, mail, etc., They brought some down, and we all went up next morning after some more. While we were there the plane came in again and we had to take off our pants and wade in water to our hips to unload him. Our District Engineer came in on it and returned to camp with us. I had ten pounds spuds, 20 lbs. sugar, 10 lbs. bacon, 8 lbs. shortening, a 12 lb. package and the rest of the sack full of oranges and onions. I felt 4 inches shorter by the time I got to camp. The District Engineer didn't know where Fred was and stayed in camp until he came back, four days later, having been eating only moose for a week.

So long
Willis

Hunting was not without other casualties as well. Ken Strawn had worn his favorite pair of pants on the hunts and managed to get them very bloody in the process. Knowing cold, not hot, water was best for blood stains, he tied them to a root where they would soak in the creek. Two or three days later he retrieved them, only to find the fabric completely destroyed, literally coming apart in his hands. This was a serious blow, since replacements were impossible to come by.

August 3 found us out of eggs, butter, fruit, potatoes, bacon, soup, flour, sugar, shortening, and much more. Fifteen men eating primarily sheep and moose. Ray the cook claimed he was inventing such things as goosie moosie, juicy moosie, and several other moosie things more or less unrepeatable. A few canned prunes and about a quarter of a case of shrimp was all that was left of the canned goods.

All this time Fred was trying to make some contact with headquarters. It seems all the planes flying over were busy moving crews beyond the White River and we were far down on the priority list. Maybe as low as our morale about that time. Finally while Fred and the pack string were twenty miles beyond us at Pickhandle Lake waiting for a plane, one came over our camp, circled into the valley above, which contained a rather sizeable lake, then promptly left. A few hours later he came back and went out of sight for about 45 minutes, then flew back out of the valley and over camp. This indicated to us that help had arrived and cargo had been unloaded.

Deciding not to wait for the pack string, we went up to the lake, where we found food and mail. Another planeload came in next day while we were there, and we packed out enough to enable a crew to be put to work. Along with this second load came John MacGillvray, district engineer, just to see how we were getting along. In order to get him ashore, Jack Edwards and I waded out hip deep into the lake and brought him out with a cross-hand carry and set him ashore.

Two days later Fred and the packers returned from their ten day safari in search of supplies. They had been subsisting on a moose harvested by the packers. He was pretty well worked up and when he found MacGillvray was in camp he really unloaded on him. When Jack and I told Fred we had carried Mac ashore, he said "Why didn't you drop the —— in the lake?"

I had never met Mac before and felt sort of sorry for him in such a hostile environment. He stayed in our tent and I had a chance to visit with him a bit. We had many mutual acquaintances, since he had been engineer on the Santiam Highway construction on Oregon for many years. This was my home country. In later times, both that winter and then in 1949 I worked with him a number of times and always got along well. We even shared a couple of times being lost in the dark in the Coast Range and Cascade mountains curing the 1950's. He passed away in 1987 at the age of 90.

After all the problems and difficulties at this camp we named it Starvation Lake camp and the creek Hard Luck Creek on the plot of our survey. These names survive on the current Geological Survey maps of Canada.

For the most part, moving camp went well, with each man knowing his job and doing it with a full awareness that if he didn't it meant a night out in the open at best or that plus rain. Best elapsed time for setting up the four tents and cookhouse was probably about two hours from the time of arrival of the horses. At each move it was the responsibility of each man to have his gear ready to be packed when he left camp for work in the morning, then the packers could load and be at the new campsite with the first load by the end of the day. Camp could then be set up at the end of the short work day.

The biggest problem move came at the crossing of the Donjek River, a major glacial stream with its source well back in the St. Elias mountains. Complicated by the fact that it was necessary to cross at the widest and shallowest point was the need to split the crew in order to project the line across the 1650 foot wide mouth of the canyon, then return with the horses to move the remainder of the crew. It was impossible for a man to cross the river on foot. Our packers were continually talking about the interrelation of hot days, rain, and quicksand in what seemed an effort to intimidate us regarding the hazards ahead.

For this move we divided the camp equipment, carrying just enough to get to the other campsite, allowing for one night in the open without shelter. The need for saddle horses for the whole crew to cross the river made it necessary to reduce the number of pack animals to a minimum.

The weather had been warm, so the glaciers were preparing a reception for us by a fast melt and high water. To aid in this, that night it rained hard, helping yesterdays sunshine to raise the river and assuring a wet crew whether or not they ever went in the river. The high water meant one more day on the open bar, already wet, and with the cook under somewhat of a strain. He hadn't brought along enough food to last that long, and was out in the rain cooking over the open fire.

Before we had left Burwash Landing, Gene Jacquot had

given a big black husky to the cook to keep him company during the course of the survey, thus relieving some of his fears about bears and other wild things. This dog was his constant companion and probably his closest confidant, and, most important,he never talked back to Ray. Right now, in the middle of running short of food and cooking over an open fire in the rain, his furry companion all at once took on a new identity. Here was the cook's opportunity to get out of this miserable job and shift the responsibility to somebody besides himself. All at once in the middle of cooking the evening meal he stood up, threw down his spoon and burst out in a tirade "That does it, I've had it, they can take this country, this place, this weather, this job, and all that goes with it and shove it, I'm going back to where I can get a plane out of here, and I'm going to do it now" With that, he packed up the dog and prepared to start out, with only his black canine friend as companion and guide for the thirty miles to Burwash Landing.

Fred had crossed the river two days earlier with the first section and wasn't there to deal with the situation. He had left Lowell Jensen in charge and right then Lowell found himself unable to soothe Rays troubled spirit.

In the interests of self preservation we all took part in the discussion, offering all kinds of help and sympathy, aimed at both keeping the cook on the job and saving him from his own folly in striking out into the bush where he had thus far only ridden a horse on the moves.

I offered to help him with meal preparation and serving, some of the others offered to go back to the camp and bring up more food, and others prepared to build him a shelter better than the rest, despite the likelihood only one more day would see us across the river. Finally he agreed to unpack the dog, pick up his spoon, squat before the fire and finish cooking supper, satisfied that he had our attention. All promises were kept, and the night was spent with reasonable assurance there would be breakfast in the morning.

Finally on the third day out all things were favorable and we made the crossing with only a reasonable amount of difficulty.

Jimmie Joe and Sam Johnson, our packers, had warned

us of possible quicksand, and, sure enough, about halfway over, with my horse about halfway between walking and swimming, suddenly he went down by the stern with a sudden lurch. In a cowardly move, I hung onto the saddle horn with both hands, and managed to stay on board. I had reason to be glad I had been riding more than some who had not had the opportunity to do so. So much for the benefits of volunteering.

After climbing out of the river we traveled about four more miles on a faint trail to the new campsite, where Fred and the others of the advance group had been impatiently awaiting our arrival for the last three days. As should be expected, he was in an elevated state of emotion and was somewhat critical of what he thought we had been doing during the time apart. Once all the facts were in and he grasped the reasons for the delay, things settled back into the normal pattern of setting up and preparing for the work ahead. Things really weren't quite normal just yet, though, it was still necessary for the pack string to return for the last load.

This campsite was the best of the season going in, with a lake, firewood, flowing stream and meat in the form of Dall sheep plainly visible on the green hill 2000 feet above the camp.

The third and last trip for the pack string was another set of problems, and this time Tom Kirkwood went with the packers, a little to my consternation. Little did I know that I was being given much the best of the situation.

Back to the camp on the Donjek they went, all 21 horses, and packed up without incident, even making the river crossing easily in cool and cloudy weather. Once across and highly visible from the air in the open meadows, who should come flying over, low beneath the cloud cover, but our old friend Les Cook, in the yellow Norseman which did so much for the PRA all that summer. Les, apparently in a more playful mood than usual for him, decided to come back and take a look, greeting the boys on the ground with a low and loud fly-by. This was too much for the horses, even our relatively well trained-group. It was Jimmie and Sam's practice to only lead one horse, and the rest were well trained to follow, without any lead rope, all trusted and able to seek their own path through the brush if need be. This time they sure did seek their own path through the brush. Scattering in all directions from the roar of the big yellow bird, they ran into trees, scattered packs, bent back the tops on the cook stoves, and generally raised havoc with the best tied packs. Two even hid so well they weren't found until the third day. Lots of work for the packers and everybody else.

This whole caper set things back a bit and was a sign of things to come to further justify the name of Hard Luck Creek for the campsite.

A little body and fender work on the bent back stove tops rendered them reasonably flat and usable, and the hard panniers had protected the food and other supplies in this last load. Fortunately most of the personal gear had been brought over in earlier loads, and the tents survived virtually unscathed.

All this stress on the cook increased his uneasiness, and as soon as he got to camp he had told Fred he was going out on the first plane. He almost did. Unfortunately for him and fortunately for the rest of us, the first plane was the one at the lake about two miles up the hill from camp. The next time around he was ready, but by then we were in much better shape to deal with his abdication.

It always seemed to be raining when I was working with the packers, but the action was enough to keep us warm. A favorite of Sam's was to roast a moose rib beside the fire, hanging it on a stick in the ground while we worked. This and a cup of tea for lunch and who could ask for more. A little grease on the fingers and face, but tasty.

Our sixth camp was on a tributary of Lake Creek, and we dubbed it Beaver Dam hotel from the dams nearby. A nice dry site in large trees, and not too many mosquitoes. The survey line was run through the camp and across this creek close to the date of my birthday, August 13, so the draftsman labeled it **Grafe Creek** on the map in recognition. This name, like Hard Luck Creek, remains yet today on the geological survey maps of the area.

Throughout nearly all the distance covered by our survey there was an underlying layer of volcanic ash several feet thick, the fallout from the volcanoes of the St. Elias range. This layer is an effective insulator, only allowing thawing to a shallow depth wherever it was deposited. Only where it had been washed away in the stream beds did the ground thaw to a depth of more than one and a half or two feet. As a result there was standing water over much of the area, lying at the base of the grass hummocks and making wet walking along with uneven footing. Every little pool among the "niggerheads" was a potential mosquito breeding spot. When it became necessary to dig holes for the garbage or latrine at the campsites, it was only possible to go down about 16 or so inches, then the shovel would hit solid and impermeable ice. Early in the season it was slow, difficult work to pound a steel bar or "frost pin" into the ground to make way for the wooden survey stakes. Slight thawing of the ground during the setup of the transit and level made accurate surveying difficult as well and required constant checking of the stability of the instruments.

At the Starvation lake, Hard Luck Creek camp it was possible to use the reasonably comfortable lake water for swimming and bathing, an unaccustomed luxury. This was fine so long as it wasn't necessary to stand on the bottom. Right beneath the foot or so of loose, muddy organic material was a flat and solid underlying layer, none other than our old friend permafrost, insulated from above by the long accumulation of leaves, needles, and fine mud. The lake water was warmed by long holding in the lake of its source above camp and the two mile trip down the hill to us, and the frost underneath was insulated enough to keep it from cooling below a tolerable level.

Three or four of the crew were smokers, and they had left Whitehorse, then Burwash Landing, with a somewhat limited supply of tobacco. By the time we were ready to move from our second camp at Long Lake to Murray Creek., a resupply became critical. Probably "desperate" would be a more descriptive word. At any rate, when the time came to move camp they launched an intensive search for old butts which might not have served out their full life. It was amusing and at the same time a bit pathetic to see grown men frantically looking through the dust around the campfire and tent sites, seeking for just one more butt whose contents could be stripped out into their nearly empty pouches.

In the running of the survey line, the most responsible and demanding position is out front, flagging the route along

44

which the work is to be done. Drainage, grade, exposure, and ease of construction must all be considered. The party chief is always responsible for this route selection. The axemen, locally hired prospectors or trappers, were in close contact with the party chief or his designate and were charged with responsibility to follow him and clean out the trees and brush so the work could proceed.

Our axeman or "bushman" as the job was sometimes designated, was Tom Kirkwood, a local prospector and all around outdoorsman. He was conscientious and hardworking, always giving his best to the job. On at least one occasion he found himself out front without a leader, but kept on working, brushing out a line which was later determined by higher authority to be unusable. He was greatly offended when called back and redirected on a new course. His pride was suffering from wounds difficult to conceal, both vocally and attitudinal. Finally Fred realized what was afoot and gave him some counsel which may well be used in many other situations. "Look, Tom" he said "it all pays the same, and if you're told to cut brush between the cook house and the outhouse all day, that's where you're supposed to work". This put things into proper perspective and settled the matter for the rest of the season.

After we left Burwash Landing there was no opportunity to acquire any kind of clothes, including shoes, socks, pants, or anything else. These items all began to show signs of wear at an early date, even though washing was kept at a minimum to avoid wear. The constant whipping of the brush as we forced our way through it was particularly wearing for those of us on the "topog" party, since we had about four times as much brush to push through and no cleared line like the others. I had worn my overalls (blue jeans today) to where there were patches on patches, salvaged from unneeded pockets or sections cut off the leg below the tops of my sixteen-inch boots. Finally I gave up on them and used a pair of riding breeches (choke bores) which I had brought along as an afterthought. Here the high boots came in handy. These were great for riding, but hot and tight for walking. The crown of my army type campaign hat wore out along the ridges from using it as a shield while stooping to go through the low bushes.

45

The water puddles on the permafrost kept our feet constantly wet, and greasing boots by the fire was an almost daily ritual. Boot grease became in short supply early on and kitchen grease soon substituted. This was a bad choice. Bacon grease was particularly bad, probably due to the salt. Rather than preserve as salt is supposed to do, it damaged the leather, causing rapid deterioration. At least that was our impression, although it may be that the leather just gave up from old age and abuse.

Walking through the permafrost areas, both dropping into the puddles and through the moss in timbered areas, caused the edges of the soles on both sides and the toes of boots to wear out at a rapid rate, sometimes clear back to the stitches.. The volcanic sand suspended in the moss was a strong abrasive against which the leather soles and uppers didn't have a chance. My boots ended up having a tin can metal cap nailed directly into the front of the sole to save the toe of the uppers. Even so, our boots had holes through the outer layer of the toes. Light rubber boots just didn't have enough support for safe walking over the hummocks.

My sister Louise was teaching at Petersburg, Alaska, and I had asked her to send me some outdoor and winter clothes by mail, which was the only dependable way. The headquarters in Whitehorse never did make any arrangements to purchase clothing or anything else for the field crews, I guess presuming it shouldn't be necessary. It may not have been for most, but we were out for a longer time and more remote than any other crew, and were in a greater state of need.

Early in the season I had asked Dad to send me my cork boots and some wool socks by mail as well.

When we moved from Grafe Creek to Pickhandle Lake the last week in August I finally got shoes, grease, boots, pants, and finally on the third load, some wool socks. Preparations for the past summer were finally complete.

While we were camped at Beaver Dam Hotel on Grafe Creek, a plane flew over very low, circled, and dropped a weighted white object. We presumed it to be a message of some sort and spent nearly five hours looking before finding it lying in the creek. It included instructions to reduce the accuracy of some aspects of our survey and speed things up to assure completion at the earliest possible date.

As a result of this, our next move to Pickhandle lake, the seventh of the season, was the last to move all the gear. After that we had to leave everything except sleeping bags and one small bag each, three flys, the two little cookstoves, and enough cooking gear to get by on to cook the selected groceries. It was by that time late August and the nightly temperature was near freezing.

When the first plane came in to our Pickhandle lake camp, Ray the cook was in a good mood and no demand to leave was made. In a few hours, however, he had heard the news of contractors working in good camps with big pay and other fine things we could not match at our camp. This precipitated an outburst and demand for passage out. Some thought he had fortified himself for the confrontation with the assistance of the vanilla bottle. He may have. Anyway, next plane in, out he went. Who should end up in the cook tent but Sam Johnson, the Indian packer, and me. Sam had done a bit of cooking for Jacquots hunting camps out of Burwash, and I had been around the kitchen a bit since age 8, so maybe we were as well qualified as anyone else. Anyway, we were the only ones not given the opportunity to decline.

The first plane in also brought a young man carrying orders for Fred to use him to replace Lowell Jensen. After some discussion with both the young man and Harvey the pilot, Jensen stayed and the young man returned whence he came. Fred had been through too much to get to where we were, and did not take kindly to what he considered arbitrary orders.

The primary purpose of the construction of the Alaska highway in the war years was to serve as a supply link to the string of airports in Canada which were on the ferry route to Fairbanks and the USSR. All through the season we saw these planes flying over, and on occasion they would come directly over the camp, although we were pretty well concealed in the trees.

Not so at Pickhandle Lake. Here camp was situated on a point of land fairly well out in the lake and well exposed, the white tents visible for miles from the air. Our allies in their P-39 Aircobras and A-20 bombers seemed to take great delight in swooping over us in low formation, seemingly almost to sight in on the stovepipe of the cook tent.

These pilots were for the most part recent graduates of flight school, and must have enjoyed the opportunity to make a mock bombing or strafing run.

Once we were ready to move camp from Pickhandle lake to the Koidern river, it was up to Sam and me to pack up just enough food out of our supplies for the last two weeks of the survey. The rest was left for our return and evacuation as soon as the White River was crossed.

Cooking under the open fly with no way to keep things warm except in the oven or on the stoves caused some problems. This was particularly true when trying to bake bread with the dry yeast available to us. It was necessary to keep the sponge warm all through the near frosty night if any edible bread was to be achieved. The only way found to beat this problem was to get it all warm and put it into one of the panniers (pack boxes), and wrap the whole thing with many layers of the horse blankets. The most exciting thing in the morning was to open up this little package and discover how much horse hair and sweat had infiltrated the bread as the sponge had risen overnite. It never got bad enough to affect the taste or color, but might have been a bit of a problem for someone neither hardy nor hungry enough to ignore it. There were no volunteers stepping forth for the job of cook, no matter what we did.

Baking bread in the little sheet metal stoves was enough of a challenge in the best of conditions, with no thermometer and a firebox and oven about the same size, only separated by a thin wall of steel. Most of the time the bread would brown well on top while retaining its pale complexion down in the pan. Once it had taken its set and wouldn't fall, however, it was simple enough to knock it out of the pan, turn it upside down, and finish the job. Any complaints from the customers were ignored.

Fred took over the bread baking job one time when we got back to Pickhandle lake for the two days we were there waiting to be evacuated. he complained to me "the holes in yours are too big, it leaks jelly". By then the pressure was off, anyway, and he needed something to do while we waited.

The breakfast pancakes, eggs, and bacon were standard, but waste could not be tolerated. The extra pancake dough would get a couple more eggs, a bit of sugar and flavoring and some raisins, becoming loaf cake for the lunches. Not too good, but not too bad, either.

A unit of the 29th Army Engineer regiment, doing similar reconnaissance work as ours, caught up with us as we were completing our work. They were out of food. I took their packer and two horses back to our camp on Pickhandle, where we restocked their larder. So much for the glory of the Army. They had administratively been determined to rely on "C" rations and apparently didn't quite come out even. They also shared in the sheep we brought off Pickhandle mountain. Their crew was armed with a couple of Ml Garand rifles which were much superior to our arms and a big help in supplying meat.

The long daylight hours were a real benefit during the summer months. We were at 62 degrees north latitude and the long work days, moves in rainy weather, and all the rest would not have been possible if the approach of darkness had been an additional limitation on the days.

Fred realized I wanted to be in on the finish of the line and see the White River, so he let me have a day out of the cook fly. We made the final tie-in of the surveys across the river at the proposed bridge site to where Del Earley's crew had started their lines a few weeks before. It was necessary to triangulate across the turbulent, glacier-fed stream at the mouth of the canyon.

The horse crossing was far downstream where the channels were wider and shallower. It was a bit of a repeat of the Donjek crossing, but with a different cast. J. H. Tucker, our 58 year old 5' 6" levelman needed to cross, since the elevations needed to be taken looking both ways across such a long span. Not a horse lover, he didn't think much of the idea, and only confirmed his fears when his horse slipped just as they were climbing the far bank and he had a close call with a free float down the icy stream. When time came to go back he told Fred "Not me, I'm not getting back on that horse" "Well Tuck," says Fred, "it's a big and deep river, and I don't know how else you're going to get across if not on the back of this broomtail" Finding himself in a box, Tucker reluctantly mounted the horse, hanging on for dear life, and the crossing was made, this time without mishap.

So ended the survey.

The final engineers station was 3,990, or just a little short of 75 miles in the four months since we had started out five miles south of Burwash Landing.

Rain delayed us one day in returning to the Pickhandle lake camp, so the completion celebration was set back accordingly.

That evening after the move back and all work was complete, Tucker dug deep into his bag and retrieved a quart of scotch Whiskey, the only alcoholic beverage anyone had seen since leaving Whitehorse. This explained why he had always been so fussy about his baggage when the packers were loading up. He and Fred and two or three others managed to put the booze to good use in properly celebrating the importance of the occasion.

It was indeed a happy time for Fred. He had been through more than the rest of us, with the worry and concern on top of all the daily difficulty of operating a survey. This is why the cooking became therapy to him. Not only did he insist on taking over the bread-baking duties immediately that night, but decided to bake pumpkin pies as well. He did a creditable job, too, all the while reciting *The Shooting of Dan McGrew.*

The supplies and personal gear at Pickhandle Lake camp had been disturbed in our absence. Only the Army had been in the area, and apparently the Colonel's men had taken the liberty to do a midnight requisition. Some dialogue took place between Fred and him later but nothing was resolved. I found my five new pairs of wool socks missing. Nothing too good for the boys in the service, I guess.

From Pickhandle lake we were scheduled to fly back to Burwash Landing, so sat tight, awaiting transport.

The only plane assigned to us was a Fairchild 74, Pat Callison pilot, plane registry #CF BXD.

About noon of the first full day back at the lake, the plane came in and Fred, Lowell Jensen, Tucker, and Harry French went out. Not much capacity for anything else. It rained hard that night, with low overcast next day, so our transport was grounded. The Air Force was still flying, though and kept life interesting by buzzing our camp.

Next day four more men went out. This time Pat brought in some mail and word that we were going to be working out of a camp west of Burwash Landing for a couple of weeks, traversing the Army road. There was a 35 mile section which needed to be surveyed in order to locate it on the map in relation to our work.

Day four was a busy one with four loads going out, with me and a lot of baggage on the third one.

The plane was heavily loaded and we taxied slowly far down the lake, then turned for the takeoff run. It seemed forever to me before Pat got the floats to plane, but we finally made it airborne, clearing the trees by camp by an adequate, if not great elevation. He cruised the plane at about 75 MPH, just above the treetops, gradually gaining altitude as he used up fuel.

After about five months of moving around only by walking or horseback, it was a thrill for me to fly over all that country and be able to identify the landmarks. I could find Grafe Creek, Quill Creek, the Duke and Donjek Rivers, and see the army road to where it had been built to within about ten miles of Pickhandle lake. Dramatic changes in a short time. We looked for the pack string which was on its way back, but never located them.

This time the landing on Kluane lake was on water and no mishaps of any kind. One more load and all our gear and people were back at the point of beginning.

Things were not the same at the Landing. The Army and contractors had left marks on the isolated little trading post, early indications of the drastic changes to come in the years ahead.

Absent any provisions having been made for quarters, five of us pitched one of the tents, built a fire, and set up housekeeping. All the neighborhood Indians gathered around and we sang and visited for a while until the locals suggested having a dance. It seemed a good idea, but somehow we weren't comfortable with things and went back to our tent. Indians and liquor don't mix, and besides, it was illegal and we couldn't afford to risk any involvement.

Two RCMP troopers were temporarily at the landing when we arrived, but left after a couple of days. We never did find out what the problem was, but guessed it might be the relationship between the natives and Army.

Next day everybody but me took off for Whitehorse, so I spent the day with the PanAm radiomen. Hughie Stone had been having trouble sighting in the gun I had sold him in the spring, so I took care of it for him.

The next morning I woke with snow and ice on my bed and the thermometer at 12 degrees. The smoke hole in the tent had let in the 1/2 inch of snow which had fallen in the night. It warmed up during the day and never dropped that low again while we were in the area for the next three weeks.

Cecil Lacy, Pat Callison, Pickhandle Lake

CAMP AT DRY MEADOW

The crew started filtering back from Whitehorse next day and we set up camp at Dry meadow, about ten miles west of Burwash. Fred went up the road to look for our packers, who were bringing the horses back from Pickhandle Lake. He finally located them at the Donjek River. While he was gone we cut wood for the tents and cookhoulse and generally prepred to start work.

When he returned he didn't see the woodpiles right away and was upset with us. The big pile behind the cookhouse finally mollified him. To me had fallen the job of sawing much of the wood, since I was the only one left in camp who could solo on the crosscut saw.

Sam Johnson and I again fell heir to the cooking duties, but this time we had the big stove which had remained behind when we moved into camp in the spring. Fred had a warm discussion with Gene Jacquot about the stove, finally convincing the trader we really hadn't traded the big stove for the two little ones. It was a fine stove, well able to heat the cook tent and bake without the need for turning the loaves of bread. We tried to keep the top smooth enough to fry meat, but never quite succeeded.

Fred christened the stove by baking the first bread. His recipe for 12 loaves ended up 21. Pretty good increase and a real saving on flour.

Work to be done from this camp consisted of tying our survey to the constructed road near our springtime point of beginning east of Burwash and traversing it for about 35 miles to where the lines once more intersected. In addition, we laid out an airstrip 8000 by 600 feet to include the grass field so laboriously hacked out by the Jacquot brothers. This one, in contrast to the original, was oriented to eliminate the need for the pilots to compensate for the 30 degree crosswind which had plagued the earlier strip.

There was some controversy over the relative merits of the two locations, but the Army, being in control of policy, won out. There was, in fact, much to be said for their location, although it was six miles longer. They had kept close to Burwash Creek and the Kluane River and followed an area with better drainage and much easier to construct. We had surveyed the area in a much more direct line, early in the summer, and found it satisfactory at that time. Unfortunately, with the advancing season, it proved to be largely on permafrost, very unstable, and difficult to drain. In the beginning there was consensus about our surveyed route, so it was not a matter of fixing responsibility. Fred ruefully commented that permafrost wasn't part of the problem in California where he was accustomed to work, so he had not realized its significance.

Except for that short portion of our seventy miles of line, the entire distance was ultimately utilized as the adopted and designed route. Initially the Army crossing of the Donjek River was upstream over a mile. The 1943 construction by our contractors was just downstream from the original, but the location across the wide, braided channels could not be maintained. The changing channels made it impossible to keep the river under the wooden trestles, and the spans were continually damaged or destroyed by scour and drift. Several bridges were initially built across the several channels. The permanent bridge finally constructed by the Canadians in the 1950's was 1650 feet long with 13 steel truss spans, and was located on our survey a couple of miles downstream at the mouth of the canyon.

Working from a good camp beside the road, no permafrost, no mosquitoes, and a dependable supply of food were all welcome changes, but a little anti-climactic to the pioneering work of the rest of the season. No complaints were to be heard. Even the dust of the occasional truck along the road was not enough to cause grumbling.

I welcomed the opportunity to work with Sam, and considered our relationship to be a good one, he freely sharing his viewpoints and thinking on many issues of life. His impressions were fascinating to hear, a mixture of his isolated life and information gained from the hunting camps of the wealthy Americans with whom he had guided for Jacquot.

Somewhere he had experienced the duplicity of the white man, and he expressed it in a rather straightforward way "Is easy way to be sorry" "White man do bad things, then say "Im sorry" and that make it all right. Then he do

54

bad thing again, same way." Somehow he felt that such an expression of regret really wasn't too sincere. I could only agree.

Another time he asked Fred "You ever see so many cars and trucks before?" as we regarded the occasional Army 6x6 Studebaker trucks passing in front of camp. "You have this much trucks where you live?" Thinking of his home in San Mateo, Fred replied, "Sam, there are more cars within a quarter of a mile of my house than there are in the whole damn Yukon".

Our first exposure to Sam was memorable for his unknowing name dropping. The big world beyond the landing was beyond his grasp, as was the concept of the number of people in other places. "You know Rockefeller?" was one of his first questions, brought on by his acquaintance with the man in question while serving as a hunting guide. His one-upmanship was totally unconscious, and there was no reason to think he was putting us on. We admitted we had heard of but never made contact with his friend, and accepted our povincialism.

Both Jimmie Joe and Sam had Model 70 Winchester rifles, Cal. 30-06, given to them by grateful hunters after a successful trip. Only Jimmie had his along, and it always seemed to be out of camp when we needed game. These were fine guns, the latest state of the art, and far beyond what any of us could have afforded at home.

The crew always carried their lunches, so we cooks had a rather large block of time in the middle of the day to use as we chose. On one occasion we went for a walk up the road to see the sawmill operated by the 18th Engineers, busily sawing out bridge plank and other smaller boards and timbers. Sam had never seen a mill other than the little one at Burwash, and thought it might be of interest to him, as it indeed was. The biggest impression of the day, though, was mine when we flushed a covey of blue grouse or "fool hens". They were new to me, but not Sam. He promptly picked up some rocks and began to throw at them. He hit a fine fat one, which promptly laid down and gave up. Sam quickly seized it and pulled off the head. We had chicken for lunch while everybody else ate sandwiches.

There was a wide, open meadow just across the road

from the camp, and now that the transit and level with their telescopes were in camp each night, we occasionally looked at the stars on the cool, clear Indian summer evenings. Sam took an interest in this operation, carefully studying the moon and stars. One night Bill Ash said to him "Sam, you know the moon is 300 thousand miles away, that's a long ways. Yes, and the earth is round like the moon, too." Sam was impressed, quietly shaking his head and murmuring. Later Tom Kirkwood and I were with him and his feelings finally came to the surface. "I don't understand about how far the moon, but if Ash says it is so, it must be so, he's pretty smart man" "If that's true, there sure must be big moose up there." This was more than we could stand and Tom asked "What do you mean Sam, about big moose up there? Sam was slow to reply, but finally came out with his concern.

"One time big chief find himself outside the sky. He wander around all over and couldn't find his way down. Finally he shoot moose, skin him out. Then he cut thongs from hide and tie 'em together to make long rope. He chop a hole in the sky, tie one end of the string to a star and let himself down to the ground. If it's that far up to the sky must be big moose to make enough thong"

We were in no position to argue with that one, it would take a big moose.

Music in our survey camp had ben confined to Cecil Lacy and his harmonica. Now, Tom Kirkwood brought his "Gramophone" from Whitehorse. The first impact of some old familiar tunes was somewhat emotional to me, almost causing a wave of homesickness. Those who had gone on in to town had taken the edge off their isolation, but when it hit me in the quiet of relatively familiar surroundings, it had a real impact. Of course, the music at the "Burwash Bounces" was also a nostalgic experience, but then the choice of records had been different and the time away from home not quite so long.

Being a cooks helper had some advantages, especially when the weather was bad. I would occasionally work in the office during the midday break, computing the survey line, which was good experience. I had never done any of the office work and Ken Strawn, the computer, was always ready to let me do his work for him. I didn't mind looking up the trig functions and cranking out the calculations on the Marchant machine, at that time the latest state of the art in calculators.

Dried and powdered eggs were a staple and used for much of our cooking, a practice which has just now begun to catch on in more settled areas. The one gallon cans had excellent suggested recipes printed on the sides, enticing us to try new things. Discovering a doughnut recipe and having an oversupply of cooking oil, we decided to try our hands at deep frying. In the course of mixing the dough, we found it difficult to achieve the right consistency. By the time a proper consistency of mix had been achieved through judicious addition of critical ingredients, we had a large dishpan full of the sticky stuff. Then began the rolling, cutting, and cooking, plus sugaring, both powdered and granulated. This caper finally ended up with 48 dozen doughnuts. For several days each tent was supplied with a bucketful at all times, and there was a corresponding decrease in consumption of breakfast and supper. A few at the end of the day while getting ready to eat really seemed to take the edge off the appetites and save on the higher priced stuff.

As at the beginning of the season, we were once more supplied with fresh beef and sawed the rations off the frozen carcass on a daily basis. No refrigeration needed as October approached.

Steaks became a problem. These men's mothers had spoiled them at home and made them picky about how their meat was fried. Each man wanted his steak custom done and a little different from his companions. One small stove cooking for 15 men makes satisfaction difficult to achieve. Finally the answer came. We set out the steaks and skillets for use around an open fire and told the customers they were to have the opportunity to cook it to their taste. Most learned to enjoy "medium rare" or even less in terms of cooking time, not wanting to wait any longer to satisfy their hunger. After that, the dinner steaks were always "just right".

Each Army regiment had a full complement of medical men, and our friends of the 18th were no exception. Major Webber, a Dentist and amateur geologist, spent some interesting times with us. His practice was in Portland, Oregon, so he was able to share with some of us as a neighbor. He offered dental services to the crew and did some repairs on teeth needing attention, pedalling away on his foot powered drill. He had been on a trip up the White river to the old site of Copper city and had some samples of almost pure copper to show us. His assistance was much appreciated and a true fringe benefit in an unexpected place.

All through the summer months there had been no card playing in camp, and there may not even have been a deck of cards available. Now, however, the benefits of civilization were available and pinochle became the favorite. I had never learned to play, but soon became as addicted as the rest. Fred was the most competitive and was camp champ if such there was.

At the end of the 35 miles when time came to tie back into the original survey, the two points computed to be over 700 feet apart rather than closing as they should. Up and down the line went the transit crew, sighting on mountaintops, seeking to find any error in bearing through triangulation. All this was futile, and Fred finally was forced to take the notes in to Whitehorse and distribute the error throughout the line in conformity to accepted practice. Not a happy situation, but it was too late in the season to do more. Finally, on October 10 the survey was completed and all hands except for Jack Edwards and me made the trip back to Whitehorse for further assignment.

Jack and I moved into the contractor's camp at the Duke river and for the next week assisted in making the soil survey along our surveyed line. This consisted of digging a hole every thousand feet or where there might be a change in the underlying soil. Most cases this was easy. The permafrost was close to the surface, and wet volcanic ash on top, so the digging was quick and shallow. In creek beds where there was gravel we established the limits of the gravel where it crossed the line and moved on. Jack and I were in good walking condition and moved rapidly down the line. We always had plenty of time to have a roaring lunch fire by the time the soil specialists caught up to us.

The first day out, the Soils Engineer, Bob Simpson, from Utah, followed our lead, and when we came to end the day we went cross country through the snow-covered timber to the army road, couple of miles to the north. We arrived at our car about dark after a short walk back along the road. Next morning we left the car where we had come out of the timber, planning to follow our tracks back to the survey line.

Bob, in his new found familiarity with the country, decided he had a more direct way and chose to lead us away from the tracks of the previous day. The clouds lay low along the toe of the mountains on both sides of the broad valley, effectively blotting out any landmarks, and he gradually bore to the left until he was hopelessly confused, walking nearly parallel to the line he was seeking. When he finally realized he was having a problem, he let me redirect our path south toward the foothills. When we found the horse trail, it was simple enough to turn right and follow it to our old campsite at Murray Creek. Then Jack, too, knew where we were.

"Where do we go now" asked Bob

"Follow the trail to the line, it's easy to find"

"I'll bet you can't find it, we'd best backtrack to the car, even if it is getting late."

Fortunately, Jack came to my support and we were able to convince Simpson we could find the line. What we didn't tell him was that it was the only camp where we had ridden the horses to work for a couple of days and everything would be easy to follow. Recognizing where I was on the first crossing of the horse trail was the critical time, and I only knew where I was because of the extra work with the packers and consequent several trips over the trail.

Finally he let me lead him back to the survey line. Earlier that morning we had unknowingly crossed it in the middle of a large opening. This was easy to do; unless a survey stake happened to be exactly where you crossed, one chance in about fifty.

We finally reached the last hole of the day before, and continued up the line working for about six miles. After all that wasted energy, we probably walked close to twenty miles that day, including the six on the line.

The next day Bob decided to follow the backtrail to work, and we finished the soil survey in the early afternoon.

From that time until 1968, 26 years later, I never saw Bob Simpson again. That year he was assigned to Oregon as Division Engineer while I was there as an Area Engineer for the Portland area. When he came in to meet the staff, he shook my hand, then turned to Al Parsons, retiring Division Engineer, and said "The last time I saw this guy, he took me for a tough walk through the Yukon Wilderness." He then proceeded to tell the story as he recalled it.

One more night in the Duke River camp and early in the morning Jack and I rolled up our gear and set out for Whitehorse. We built a fire beside the road and finally managed to get a ride in an Army ambulance to Kluane (Silver City) at the south end of Kluane Lake. There I slept on the counter of Hayden's abandoned store labeled **USO Headquarters**, while Jack made his way on toward Whitehorse. Traveling alone had some advantages, allowing for a lot more independence and flexibility.

The next day it was out to the road again, where I got a ride in an Army truck, arriving at PRA headquarters in Whitehorse about 5 PM. Nobody was expecting me, but in a couple of hours I located my stored gear and settled in in the big bullpen bunk room.

Thus came full circle the 1942 work in the western Yukon which had started in April.

The surveys to the west that year were all completed by that time, although both the Army and civilian construction forces continued to work on road and bridges clear until freezeup.

The test of time has shown the competence of the work done. In the many subsequent years, the Canadian Army and civilian contractors have continued to improve the road to where it is now a modern highway with well engineered curves and grades.

In 1983, forty years after the major portion of the work was completed, I was privileged to revisit those portions of the location on which I worked. John Hudson, Public Works, Canada, Whitehorse, at that time asked me why the original road was so crooked. I could only tell him that was how the army built it and they wouldn't let us straighten it out because late in 1943 they panicked and thought we couldn't build it in time as we had designed. Nobody will ever know if they were right, but there were, and are, differences of opinion.

Mr. Hudson was very complimentary of our work. He said that as they developed their plans for reconstruction of

60

the highway it was possible, almost without exception, to utilize our basic design and location, and found the route needed little if any modification.

Once our crew got to Whitehorse, it was dispersed to several different locations for temporary assignments or the winter. Fred, Tucker, and Harry French were the only permanent employees, and went back to California for the winter. There they worked on design of the road to be built in 1943.

I went over beyond Watson lake to a camp on Contact Creek, where we worked on finishing a location for the Fort St. John District.

Pan Am Radio Station, Burwash. Operators Gordon Warren; Hugie Stone, with Archie Erickson

On the town in Whitehorse. Kelly, Hill, Ash, Kirkwood, Bassett

Looking for Bucket Wood

EAST FROM WHITEHORSE

The PRA office I returned to in Whitehorse was a far cry from the quarters of April, and it was almost with culture shock that I viewed the changes which had taken place.

Southeast of the center of town, near to the base of the hill below the airport, stood a complex of brown wood frame, single story buildings. The unmistakable characteristics of a semi-permanent military installation were evident in the long, narrow wings, extending north and south for eight or ten rows, interconnected by enclosed walkways forming a repeated "H" pattern. It reminded me of the Civilian Conservation Corps camps at home in Oregon, except that the buildings there had not been interconnected. Later I found that they had, indeed, been previously used for some similar activity before being dismantled and shipped north for our use.

Inside their long, narrow confines was the entire headquarters operation of the Whitehorse Division, with authority extending from Watson Lake, on the east to the Yukon-Alaska border on the west, beyond what would become the village of Beaver Creek. 853 miles, over half the entire 1570 miles of the Alaska Highway were under the jurisdiction Frank E. Andrews, the Division Engineer, from Portland, Oregon.

In contrast to the springtime effort which was devoted to launching the location surveys, the entire emphasis had now shifted toward design and construction, with some contractors already working, improving the army road all across the division. The pioneer road was being prepared for the 1943 season and in the process being upgraded to assure passage during the coming winter and spring.

The north end of the front wing of the building complex, closest to town, contained the administrative and engineering offices, including survey, design, and bridge sections. In the south end were the accounting and other support staff. Two of the south wings contained the PHS Hospital, where Dr. Doyle and staff provided medical services to all the PRA and contractors personnel in the division.

Beyond the mess hall the farthest east wings had been

63

set aside as shop, motor pool, and warehouse, and all the remaining wings were taken up with quarters for personnel, both permanent and transient.

The barracks buildings had a central hallway with single rooms along each side, each about twice the size of the bed. Wonder of wonders, there were now women present, clerical and secretarial support staff to assure that the correspondence and accounting were done right and the administrators looked good at the next level.

Into all this sophisticated society I came, finding myself all at once surrounded by four wooden walls, a roof, doors, and windows, and wonder of all, hot showers on demand.

As itinerant personnel I was quartered in a large room in one wing, capable of bunking about forty men. This was more than adequate for the short turnaround time for the field men. Two days was a long stay, considering the continuing high need for men out along the construction projects and surveys.

I arrived late on Saturday and was assigned a bunk in the "bull pen" as the large room was termed. Sunday off, then over to the survey office to report to J.B. Reher for reassignment. Here it was discovered the Ft. St. John Division had come upon troubled times in completing their surveys and needed some help from our Division to finish tying things together before the icy blasts of winter made work impossible.

Accordingly, Tuesday morning was to be the end of the urban vacation and back to the cotton chateaus for another stint on a survey crew until the weather drove us out.

Fortunately, my sister Louise, in Petersburg, had purchased and mailed to me some reasonably presentable clothes, so I could venture out in public in respectability. My clothes of the past season were down to patches on patches. The new clothes were a stroke of great good fortune for my one night of city type socializing. In this case it was possible to pay a Monday night visit to the Whitehorse Masonic lodge, where the local members were very warm and cordial. It really wasn't too difficult to fall back into the old pattern of living, despite six months of rusted manners and a skin freshly scrubbed clean of the accumulation resulting from something less than adequate bathing facilities

Socializing done and the vacation over, Tuesday morning bright and early I was deposited at the airport on the hill, where I once more joined up with pilot and friend Pat Callison, with whom I was to fly to Watson Lake.

Starter problems on the Fairchild, then weather problems on the way to Watson Lake, so we didn't take off until 2:00 PM.

Lots of action to watch at the Whitehorse airport, with bush planes and ferry command both involved along with commercial flights. Pat struck up a conversation with a brand-new Army Air Force Second Lieutenant, fresh from flight school. They ended up comparing aircraft, the P-39 Aircobra, with its big engine burning 80 gallons of fuel an hour and our Fairchikd 74 with its 225 horsepower burning 8. It was an interesting study in contrasts. The soft-spoken, confident Pat with his long record of safe flying under bush conditions, and the brand new, self assured lieutenant, pink pants, crushed hat and all, embarked on one of his first flights out of school.

Once all was favorable we took off, bound at last for Watson Lake. Less than halfway out, near the community of Teslin, we encountered a nasty snow squall, enough to make Pat take a look at the newly graded airstrip nearby. One look was enough. Flying low above the treetops all we could see were some water-filled ruts in the mud, so on to Watson Lake, where weather finally cleared.

It was too late for Pat to return to Whitehorse that day, so his friends at the airport, Canada Transport, provided us with a good bunk for the nite. I later found Pat had operated a fleet of trucks and barges between the Stikine River village of Telegraph Creek, Dease Lake, and Lower Post during the construction of the Watson Lake airport. He seemed to know everybody whenever a need arose. Certainly he was the best of sponsors to have when you are short a bed for the night.

The DOT terminal building was an attractive, well built two story log building, the peeled logs still bright with the shine of newness. It is still in use today, fifty years later.

In the morning, after waiting for the ferry command pilots to blast off for Fairbanks with their 8 A-20s and 6 P39s,

Pat took off on his return trip to Whitehorse, leaving me to await whatever was in store.

About 10:30 a yellow PRA panel truck came in with Herb Friel, a survey party chief, and Eric Erhart, location chief for the Ft. St. John Division. They acknowledged me, then went about their business, leaving me to await developments. After about three hours of telegraphing, they loaded up a shipment of food for the survey crews and told me to jump in, they were ready to go. By dark we reached Friel's camp, about thirty miles south.

It was old home week for me to a degree. Six of the crew members had been fellow passengers in the hold of the Eli D. Hoyle the previous April, so a good bit of lie swapping was in order. This crew had been together with the same chief all season long, and were worn pretty thin. In contrast to our experience, they had had a degree of motor transport for most of the season and had been much less isolated. Despite the improved conditions, the food wasn't as good as ours had been and the crew members attributed it to the penurious attitude of their boss. Not a great morale builder when you have nothing else to do with your time but work, eat, wash clothes, grease boots, and sleep.

Overnight there, then it was southbound again for me. This time I was given a GMC panel truck to drive on down the road to my new assignment with Roy Lednicky at Contact Creek.

Here, again, it was old home week. Archie Erickson, Louis Montalva, and Hugh Kelly from my old crew were there, and I found a bunk available in their tent. The rest of the crew was reserved toward us for a while, but that was to be expected when new kids show up on the block. It's never possible to know what stories precede you or what assumptions are made about you when entering a new situation.

Our camp was beside Contact Creek, so named because here, not many days earlier, the grading crew of the 35th Engineers regiment, working north, had first met those of the 340th working south. This was the last linkup in the road in this division, leaving only a short section to the far north beyond the White River, near the Alaska border.

The campsite was a flat area on the south side of the

creek, in a dense grove of spruce and pine. It was typical of all our survey camps; four bunk tents, a cook tent, and an office, all scattered around in uncertain pattern to take advantage of the level open spots between the trees.

The survey crews from the Whitehorse division had been assigned temporarily to the Ft. St. John Division in an effort to complete the location surveys in 1942.

The rapid construction of the pioneer road by the army regiments had at times exceeded the capacities of the original crews to stay in the lead and much of the road had been located by individual PRA engineers assigned to the respective regiments. This had left a forty or fifty mile gap of unconnected survey.

The three crews under John Happala, Herb Freil, and Roy Lednicky, had, throughout the past season been leap-frogging each other through the eastern sector of the Whitehorse Division, between Teslin lake and British Columbia, so were all available at about the same time. Key people had been taken from each crew on completion of their original work, and I was one of those selected to be given a second opportunity to serve on one of them as winter approached.

Similar to the work my old crew had done after completion of the original assignment, we were surveying along the recently constructed pioneer road. In this way the gap could be closed and a map prepared for use by designers in readying plans for 1943.

In contrast to the glacial rivers and lakes of the western Yukon, I now found myself in a landscape of rolling hills, thickly forested with pine and spruce. The former covered the higher and dryer areas and the latter filled the valleys. Through all this the road pursued its winding path, up and down and back and forth, many times seeming to have no purpose or consistent direction.

High log and debris piles lined both sides of the road where the bulldozers had cleared the right of way for the grading to follow. As in my previous assignment, the new help was assigned to the cross section or "topog" crew, charged with gathering information along both sides of the transit line to enable plotting of the contour map.

In ordinary uncleared forest such as this it is normally possible to walk and see through the vegetation well enough

67

to make good progress. Unfortunately, the large log and brush piles now in place made it much more difficult, requiring constant scrambling to establish the natural ground contour.

Getting to work and back was also a problem for the first few days. The road was only a few weeks old and unsurfaced, which means muddy at that time of year, and the Army was still working to get it consistently passable. Fortunately, after about a week the temperature dropped to well below freezing, so the mud was stabilized by the weather, something even the Army couldn't accomplish.

With the colder weather and snow came other problems. Climbing over the log piles became more of a chore and more dangerous as the snow depth increased. Things were slowed considerably. The Army even helped out in their own way by wiping out three miles of survey line with their graders on one occasion, then left the country for points south, never to return. This required a whole new beginning on a section, with resultant delays.

For the topog crew in particular the cold weather brought on misery for the note keeper. Usually this job is performed by the most senior and responsible member of the crew. Not so in cold weather. Then the most active job is the most desirable and rank has its privilege. Temperatures of zero and below make barehanded writing of small numbers in a book a most unpleasant chore, so status gave way to comfort whenever deals could be worked. The final resolution of the problem came in the form of a castoff army bucket lying along the road. As in the poem *The Cremation of Sam McGee* "Here, said we, with sudden glee, is our firepot, for free". Knocking a small hole in the side of the bucket near the bottom to create a draft hole, we took some twigs and fired up, thus creating a portable finger warming fire. Not so much conflict after that over who should take notes, but the feet still got cold from standing still.

The sudden advent of really cold weather caught us more than somewhat unprepared. The standard footwear was rubber and leather pacs which just don't cut it when it drops to -20 unless you are moving around a lot. In our case it was barely adequate. Strangely enough, Phil Englebrecht, a Canadian trapper with us, was least prepared and Roy had to

Life in Camp (Author)

Crew Truck Headed South

Contact Creek Bridge

make a quick trip with him to Lower Post to get felt boots and overshoes. After that he was the only one in camp with adequate footgear.

Getting water out of frozen Contact Creek became a problem and wood enough for the six stoves took up much time, including the weekend day off. the 12'x14' tents just weren't made for such use. Neither was I. I tended to perspire, either sweat when warm or clammy when cold, and had a difficult time keeping my boots dry. Each evening it was necessary to thaw the insoles out of the shoepacs and try to dry everything out for morning. Fortunately for me, the clothes Louise had sent from Petersburg were adequate. I wore a set of cotton longjohns, a Stanfields Blue Label 100% wool union suit, a wool shirt, sweat shirt, sheepskin vest, lightweight parka, and to top it all off, a heavy wool mackinaw. Not too easy to move, but the joints didn't freeze, anyway. On two occasions white spots formed on my face and nose while walking down the road into a slight breeze at -25.

The tent stoves weren't designed with any kind of draft control, so it was impossible to keep a fire through the night. Ice all around my head each morning was normal and the hot water can hanging on the side of the stove would be partly frozen by morning, despite starting the night hot. These cans were very difficult to handle, since they hung from a wire hook around the stack, leaning against the 60 degree slant of the side of the stove. Getting them off safely was treacherous, and bailing was better if not too much was needed. It wasn't too hard to go without a bath under such conditions.

Unfortunately, on our first Sunday out Archie Erickson could no longer stand being dirty and decided, despite the difficulty, to take a bath in the big round tub. The hanging hot water can was too much for him and he spilled hot water on one leg and foot, burning them severely. Roy had to take him to Watson Lake to catch the next plane, and he never returned. After healing up in Whitehorse, he went home to San Francisco to stay.

Happala's crew finished their job a few days before we did and passed through our camp on their way back to Whitehorse.

They were once again envious of our food, along with

71

Friel's crew. They wanted to know "How did you get all this stuff, fruit, etc., everybody tells us there's nothing like this available." It seems Hap, the old Finn logger, wouldn't order anything but "Sardines and beans". When told "All you need to do is put it on the order" they harassed Hap a bit. They told us that earlier in the season they had added a bunch of items to the food order after he had signed it, and it made him furious when all that highpriced stuff came in.

Part of it, of course, was our superlative cook, Andy Isaacson, who had worked for PRA crews for many years in the northwest. He was a highly respected, no nonsense sort of guy who ordered what he needed and tolerated no editing of the sheet by anybody. He and Roy understood each other. He was truly an accommodating and understanding cook, and contributed greatly to high morale in the camp. He had early on gained the respect of the surveyors when they were setting up his cookstove, trying to level it up with their instruments. After watching for a while, he said "If you don't mind, there is an easier way that has always worked for me." He thereupon took one of his 11x13 inch biscuit pans, set it on the stove, and poured in just enough water to cover the bottom. Easy enough then to tell if it was level. Sometimes things can be over engineered.

All the time we were at Contact Creek there was much speculation as to whether we would go home via the south or north. To find out on the day before we finished, Roy Lednicky went to Watson Lake to inquire. The answer came back "Neither for now, the Peace River Bridge to the south and Nisutlin Bay ferry to the north are both out of service."

Facing the prospect of no transport for several days, Roy turned three of us loose to find our way back to Whitehorse by whatever means we could. We took off hitchhiking, with bedroll and not much else, confident that we could keep going somehow.

Only the PRA and the Army were in the area, so anywhere we would stop, quarters of some kind could be found.

I managed to get a ride about 11 AM and ended up at camp 72, East of Teslin. Imagine my surprise to find all of Haps crew plus my own crewmates, Chuck Ellis and Walt Green. Here we were given space on the sawdust floor of an Army log cabin mess hall.

The action went early and late, with the nite life just about overlapping the mustering of the cooks to prepare breakfast.

As I lay on the sawdust floor, snug and warm for the first time in a while, I suddenly realized I was hearing a familiar voice. Here, far away from home, for some inexplicable reason, KOAC, Corvallis, Oregon 550 KC, was coming in loud and clear. The northern lights have not only seen queer sights, they have done a few other strange things as well.

My rides so far had been in 6x6 Studebaker trucks, the standard vehicle for all the regiments. They were sturdy, dependable vehicles, capable of carrying 18 drums of gasoline and any other cargo necessary. Unfortunately, they had one serious drawback for arctic operation. The gas line filter sediment bulb was situated just forward of the fuel tank, low on the right side beneath the running board. Not dirt, but water in the gas was the prime difficulty. All this was brought about by the practice of storing the fuel drums on end so water could seep in through the capped filler hole and contaminate the fuel. Water at the bottom of the barrel was pumped into the tank and maintained in action long enough to stay liquid until it got to the sediment bulb. There it settled, gradually building up a block of ice in the subzero temperature. Slowly the truck would begin to starve until finally no longer able to go. Three times the first ride we stopped in the dark, cold Yukon night, unscrewed the bulb and set it afire in the road to thaw the block of ice. A little inconvenient, but worth it to long as some progress west was being made.

The problem described above became so severe as the winter progressed that the Army brought in a truckload of grain alcohol for deicing in the fuel. Unfortunately, it skidded and left the road somewhere east of Teslin and was lost for several weeks. There was much speculation as to how much this valuable beverage might have brought if the right entrepreneur could have realized its potential.

After a short night in the sawdust and a 50 cent breakfast from the Army, I caught a ride west again, this time about mid-afternoon in a standard civilian design Ford 6 dump truck, loaded with assembled stovepipe. Just like carrying

73

a lot of holes with a rim around them. Not much weight, though, which came in handy later. This rig didn't run too well, either, but we worried along with it until reaching one of Dowell Construction Co. camps, 7E from Whitehorse, about 12 miles east of Teslin. Next morning I got the camp mechanic to check it out. He found water (ice) in the distributor and poor ignition points. Once this was fixed, we set off once more.

When we came down the steep hill to Nisutlin bay, where the ferry normally ran across to the village of Teslin, we realized the full impact of the freezeup on the movement of traffic. Here the 2200 foot wide entrance to the bay was considered not yet frozen well enough for trucks to cross, and the traffic was backed up on both sides waiting for the low temperatures to do their job. Supposedly it would take nine inches of new ice to carry the trucks and the latest reading was seven. The driver and I concurred that our load of holes was lighter than standard and our truck, too, not as heavy as regular Army equipment, and decided to go on across. In the confusion we slowly drove down the ferry ramp and launched onto the ice. Not even a cracking noise, so across we went, stopping for dinner at Johnsons crossing, then had clear sailing to Whitehorse, arriving about 10 PM.

There the place was alive with action and excitement. The dedication of the road at Soldiers summit on Kluane lake was to be in two days. At last the reason for the unavailability of transport became clear. All available vehicles were commandeered to take the dignitaries and near famous to the great event. Grover Whalen of New York was supposed to have been there as a US representative, but I never ran across him. All these extra people were adding to the housing and dining problem. Whitey Goodman and his kitchen crew were doing themselves proud in caring for the multitude.

In the morning the news came in that two trucks had gone through the ice at Nisutlin bay, where we had crossed two days before. There were no survivors. Praise the Lord for a light truck and a load of holes.

Happala, Chuck Ellis from my crew, and I were assigned to launch a rescue operation for the crews stranded on the far side of Nisutlin Bay. Unfortunately for me, on the long trip out on the snowy and frozen roads I was a casualty of my own inexperience. My Dodge Screenside "Dog Wagon" was too light in the tail for my driving expertise and I failed to properly estimate my stopping distance behind an Army truck. Result: one bent nose for the Dodge and a night for me at camp 5E while Chuck and Hap completed the mission. I limped back to Whitehorse next day and parked the rig at the shop, too ashamed to go in and make my peace with the mechanics. I don't know if they ever did find out who was assigned to that truck. Fortunately for my good name, no red tape was ever reeled out on it.

Despite this evidence of irresponsibility, Hap asked me next day if I'd go to Haines for the winter to work on the construction of the Haines cutoff. It sounded good to me to be on the ocean side of the hills, so I jumped at the chance. Of course, the choice probably wasn't mine, but I could only have resigned and gone home otherwise, as an option.

Two days later our baggage was still at Nisutlin bay, or rather Teslin, so I was again dispatched to there, with a newly winterized vehicle for Harry Hedges, who was staying at the trading post at Teslin, where he was working on construction.

Teslin post was operated by the McLearys, and had been for a number of years. He was a retired RCMP trooper, and had settled there with his wife and daughters after his patrolling days were over.

Harry and his crew were using one of the buildings at the post for office and bunkhouse and taking their meals at the McLearys.

The most impressive thing about Teslin was Mrs. McCleary. She set the atmosphere for the whole establishment. The two girls were in school in Vancouver, so she was cooking for the whole crew and keeping the house without visible assistance. Despite this, the appearance and atmosphere in the dining room conveyed the feeling that a formal event was somehow in progress. The table service was English China and fine silver with full place settings. Most amazing of all, she was in every way the gracious hostess for each meal, presiding at the table dressed in a way appropriate to the finest drawing room. Mr. Mac was always well turned out in his gray flannels and fine shirt, but did not quite radiate the same glow.

It was my first exposure to what might have been the British Colonial image which carried the empire to the far corners of the world, and welcome it was as a change from the more rustic and frontier atmosphere of the past months.

Next morning my vehicle would not start, but after help from the Army and others I managed to get down to the bay, collect the errant baggage, and make my way back to Whitehorse. At last it was time for the next assignment.

The experience to the east was a great opportunity to meet a lot of new friends and gain a perception of how the rest of the world was living while we were out in the western Yukon wilderness.

From now on, motor transport would replace horses, freezeup would break up and it was time to face the future.

Chilkoot Barracks Dock

HAINES FOR THE WINTER

All the time we had been working in the interior the forces of war had brought about the recognition of a need for another route to Alaska beside the open sea and the new road. Thus was created the Haines Cutoff, so named because it would run from the Lynn Canal at Haines, 18 miles south of Skagway, up the Chilkat river, across Chilkat pass, and connect to the Alaska Highway about 100 miles west of Whitehorse.

This new route would afford a protected route for the salt water shipping all the way to Alaska, screening it with the islands of the inside passage and Alaska Mainland along the Lynn Canal. Large tows of barges could be brought to Haines, beached there at low tide, and cargo transshipped inland to Fairbanks, all without needing major seagoing vessels.

The field and office work necessary for the design of this road was getting well launched when I returned from the east, with crews to be used on both ends of the route through the winter months while construction could not be done in the interior, with its hard freezeup. The crew working in the interior was to utilize "Wanagans," buildings towed behind a tractor, for office and living quarters, while those of us who went to Haines would be quartered wherever we could find a place to live.

This was an urgent matter, and when I reported to Location Chief J. B. Reher, I was told to take the rest of the day to recuperate from the past few days and be ready to take the train to Skagway in the morning. This gave me just about time enough to retrieve my baggage from storage and take care of getting ready for the next stage of things.

Down to the station early in the morning to see the puffer billy not yet puffing and not about to for a while. The Army had taken over the railroad, brought in new engines, and was doing a creditable job, but the wear and tear on men and equipment was too much to expect predictable schedules. Anyway, after four tries and a few phone calls, we finally gave up at 9:30 PM and went back to the barracks for

77

the night We missed the train, it finally went out at 4 am without us.

So be it, nobody was all that concerned, and we caught the noon train for Skagway, arriving there after the 110 mile ride across White Pass at 10 PM. There Bob Killewich, now in charge of the transient quarters, provided us with a place to bed down for the night.

E. W. Elliott construction Co. of Seattle was operating a fleet of commandeered yachts, small boats, and other sundry craft all up and down the coast, shipping supplies and men to the Alaska projects. He had established a barracks in Skagway for such as we were, so breakfast was not too hard to come by, and we took advantage of it after the long night on the train.

Right after breakfast it was off to the customs people to get our gear through their shop and back into US territory at last. Now for transportation to Haines, only 18 miles away across the deep waters of the Lynn Canal. The schedule called for a morning departure, and it was only a little after noon when I went aboard a big, new, seagoing tug for the one hour ride across the deep blue, mountain-rimmed fjord. It was an uneventful trip, and a welcome change from the bitter cold of the interior. All the staff from Skagway was along with us, I later found out in order to attend a dance that night in the School Gym, sponsored by the survey crews. Not bad public relations.

The rain and wind were welcome after the interior, and as we docked in front of Chilkoot barracks it seemed as if I was in an entirely different world.

Directly in front of us as we approached the dock was a broad expanse of open grass, gently sloping up from the high tide line to what appeared to be an old and permanent military installation. In several locations across the sloping greensward were pits, camouflaged, yet obviously meant to represent gun emplacements. To cap it all, from where we docked, it was possible to see protruding from each pit, beneath the camouflage cover, a tree section about 8" in diameter, obviously intended to represent an artillery piece. It was not hard to see through the attempt to give the impression the fort was defended at the beginning of WW II. It seems almost ludicrous now to reflect on such fruitless efforts in the face of any real threat, but if nothing else, a certain psychological value no doubt accrued. First impressions would be important if viewed only momentarily through a periscope, but much beyond that would soon result in exposure of the real weakness of the defenses.

No official greeter was in evidence when our tug was finally docked, but the best advice was to go over to Haines, about one mile around the bay, where our PRA office was situated.

Since the baggage was still on the barge, no delays or decisions were necessary in that regard, so first available transport was accepted.

As we turned right along the road, just above the high tide line, it was possible to gain a further view of the Army post, Chilkoot Barracks, as I later learned. My first view was of an impressive row of four huge frame buildings three or four stories high, gleaming white with green trim. These were obviously barracks, and anything behind was obscured by the flattening of the slope beyond.

All this was hidden by trees as we traveled along the road skirting the bay, then turned left and up a steep hill through the center of town.

First impression was of a village suddenly awakening from a long nap. On the right, interspersed with a few houses, were Sheldon's general store, a hardware store, grocery store, the city library, a dry goods store, and at the top of the hill at the first and only intersection, the four story hotel building where the office was located. The other side of the street thus far was taken up by the Presbyterian Church, Indian mission, and farm.

The buildings were a mix of old and new, becoming progressively newer as we went up the hill. The concrete hotel building, although ill maintained, did, from a little distance, give a rather modern impression. The roots of the village as a trade route terminal for the gold rush probably accounted for the difference in age as the distance from the waterfront increased. All four stories of the hotel had been taken over by the PRA, and it was there, up the back stairway to the second floor that I reported to John Haapala, project engineer and party chief. By then it was Saturday

79

afternoon and no time was left for anything but to get settled in.

Getting established consisted of waiting around for a ride back around the bay to the barracks, which the Army had generously allowed us to use as temporary quarters. All in one room, with steel cots and steam heat. A welcome change from some of the recent past.

Getting acquainted was easy. First in the barracks, all in one room, then, despite no baggage yet off the barge, the public dance in the school gym, where the survey crews did, indeed, host the town.

There were about 20 of the PRA crewmen on board by then, including all categories, and all entered enthusiastically into putting on the dance for the locals, who turned out in force, including a few of the Indians. Even a few Army personnel from the barracks were there, the only ones in uniform. This small contingent was the caretaker and maintenance force, commanded by a Captain, and all were feeling somewhat left out of the war effort right then, but they were very accommodating to our needs.

Our engineering crew was the vanguard of the operation in Haines, and no contractors had as yet become established, so without the cooperation of the barracks commander, we would have been in a difficult position. We only occupied one squad room out of about one hundred on the base, so really weren't much of a burden. The steam heat and unlimited hot water were a welcome luxury.

Survey and design of the first few miles of the road had already been done, and we were to provide construction staking for the use of the contractor in his efforts through the winter, once he became established.

The first day on the job the snow was soft and about two feet deep, but the weather was mild. Still no baggage off the barge, but enough hand gear to get by. Finally late Monday nite all was together again in one place in the barracks.

The Army was particular about housekeeping, which is a bit difficult for dirty old surveyors, but survival instincts made it easy to adapt. After ten days of barracks life, we moved out to the town, wherever a house could be found. Meanwhile we took our meals at the bar and restaurant

80

across the street from the office and one door removed from the Mayor's liquor store.

Speaking of the mayor, he was far and away the most successful entrepreneur in the town. The liquor store was somehow always well stocked, despite the fact that on occasion the grocery shipment was late. The Alaskans seem somehow to have their own set of priorities.

Normally, survey crews on field jobs would take their meals at the contractors mess hall. In our case, however, no contractor was yet on the job, thus the need to eat at a public restaurant. For us, it was on a meal contract with PRA, to assure the men were adequately fed and not trying to save money through malnutrition. Production drops from both malnutrition and other causes. The problem can also be different when the crew stays in the bar too long after supper, socializing to the detriment of tomorrow's labors.

Heavy snowfall occurred soon after we started work, necessitating much improvisation in getting to the job up the road. The survey vehicles had not yet arrived, so we put a tent up on the back of a dump truck, using it to transport personnel with only a reasonable amount of discomfort and inconvenience. One of the larger problems was the snowdrifts which blocked the road, necessitating a lot of maneuvering by the driver as the crew sat blindly in the bed, trying to anticipate which way the next move would be.

Our location chief, John McGillvray, was also afoot, and commandeered transportation as needed. He, too used an old WPA dump truck with a greater or lesser degree of success. Probably one of the more memorable sights was the view of a big green truck coming down the road with bed in the full upright position and John with a big grin on his face at the friendly and almost hysterical reception he was getting from his crew. Fortunately for us, this never occurred when the crew was riding in the back.

After a week or so the Army requested us to move out of the barracks to make room for one of the regiments coming out of the Yukon. Instead of being provided project facilities, we were placed on a housing allowance of six dollars a day, unprecedented in the history of the PRA, which virtually never allowed cash subsistence. For this amount we could live anywhere we wished.

As a result of this action, we scattered out in town wherever we could find a place to stay. Hector Langdon and Hugh Taylor rented a house with a wood heater, and Don Reid and Cecil Pozzi moved into a two room apartment on the same floor as the office. The latter was better, even though the "Arizona" oil heater vacillated between roaring and purring. They also had lots of visitors from the upriver crew, visiting for the social events or other reasons. The big davenport carried a great variety of bodies and the troops were always welcome. Proximity to the restaurant was another great advantage in the bad weather. I later decided to move in with them after going to Petersburg for Christmas. Unfortunately, the water system in the hotel froze up in early January and didn't function for about two months. The closeness of the restaurant across the street and forbearance of the school for use of their showers still made life reasonably liveable.

On the first floor beneath us was a small soft drink bar and social center, patronized primarily by the Indians. Each night we were lulled to sleep by the jukebox booming out the latest musical hits. 1942 was the first year of "Dreaming of a White Christmas", and we dreamed well into the spring along with "Johnny Doughboy Found a Rose in Ireland," "Tangerine", and "They're Either Too Young or too Old". Any time I hear "White Christmas" I can still in my minds eye see that dark, windswept street and my minds nose can smell the spills from the oil circulator, both so vivid through that long winter.

THE TOWN AND THE PEOPLE

Located a short distance from the mouth of the glacier-fed Chilkat river, Haines is on the site of the traditional trading post for the native tribes of this portion of Alaska. The fierce and warlike Tlingit Indians held the coastal area and far upstream, exacting tribute from the less aggressive Athabaskan and Stick tribes of the interior.

It was over this old trade route, only slightly used since the advent of the white traders, that the new road was to be built.

The town showed little sign of past activity, but was for the most part in a dormant state upon the arrival of the road crews. There did not appear to be any activity except for a small sawmill and a salmon cannery at Letinkof cove, over on the river. The small grocery, hardware, general store, and liquor store appeared to be on not much more than a survival basis.

The Army contingent at the barracks consisted of only a handful of uniformed maintenance personnel, supplemented by a few civilians. Past glory was much in evidence in the form of the impressive buildings and large, well landscaped compound and drill field. The war seemed to have passed it by, at least for the time being.

There was a significant percentage of Tlingit and Chilkat Indians in the immediate area of the town, but their main settlement was several miles up the river at Klukwan. Indians were not much in evidence in the town itself except at the high school, and due to prohibition on alcohol use, did not frequent the restaurant.

Home in Haines

Start Work at Six Mile

Hardrock along the Chilkat

ENTERTAINMENT

The influx associated with the road project, first of our crews, then the buildup by the contractors, was the biggest thing to hit town since the gold rush of 1898, forty-five years earlier. Of course, then there had been nothing at the site except the buildings of the fur traders and some Indian dwellings. Now we were benefitting from a well established town which had been waiting in a void for recovery of its earlier energy. With the withdrawal of the troops from the barracks some years earlier, the biggest thing left in town had been the Presbyterian Church and Mission. Here orphaned and needy Indian children from all over southeast Alaska were educated until they could begin high school somewhere else.

The townspeople welcomed our crews and extended their hospitality in many ways. The school, church, and many individuals made a real effort to help us locate quarters when the Army was no longer able to accommodate us, and I, for one, was several times invited into the homes of the community.

Alaska being the frontier it was, the population of single women was practically zero. There were only two or three other single men on the crew besides myself, however, so the social life was not at a very high level outside the bar and restaurant, where every evening was a stand alone event.

The Saturday night dances in the gymnasium were always the high point of the week, and elicited a good turnout with no cultural or ethnic barriers. We took our turn sponsoring these events, which also helped to build community relations.

Basketball is the only winter sport in the isolated towns in Alaska, and the high school and local young men saw us as a new group of players. We did our best to live up to the challenge, fielding a team of sorts from whoever was available. Sometimes the equipment wasn't quite what todays players require, but there was never any question of effort and enthusiasm. Gym shoes were a problem, and in their absence I played in a pair of low, pull-on rubber boots, which only resulted in one sprained ankle in the whole three or four months of play.

The Indians were particularly aggressive competitors, and some of the young post-high school players were very good. A few years earlier the school had fielded a team which had placed high in the Southeast Alaska rankings, and they were still seeking to regain a bit of lost glory at our expense. On occasion one or two might come to play already fortified with fire water or some other form of anti-freeze, causing a bit of a problem until more sober heads could prevail. Not serious, but cause for a little concern, nevertheless. These games did, in their more orderly times, enable more social contact to develop between us and the townspeople.

Upon the first visit of some of us to Sunday worship, the Pastor and School Director, Rev. Knudsen, sought us out as prospective choir members, as did Miss Cora Horton, choir director and schoolteacher. The choir consisted of seven or eight ladies and the Pastor, so there was no question about his sincerity. I prevailed on Spud Canfield, one of my colleagues, to give it a try on Wed. nite. He came once, but decided to drop out thereafter. I continued on in this effort, finding it not only rewarding in and of itself, but a great opportunity to get better acquainted with a few people.

Every Sunday morning the choir would bravely sing an anthem, the ladies in the front row and the Pastor and me in the rear. He was the tenor section, I the bass. The congregation, including thirty or so mission children in the front pews, always responded to our efforts with respectful and appropriate Presbyterian silence and dignity. Whether this was an indication of spiritual worship or just longsuffering, we never had a clue.

THE JOB

The work on the Haines Cutoff as it came to be called, was divided into two sections, with our crew located at Haines itself and another at Pleasant Camp, a lodge 42 miles up the river.

Our work entailed preliminary location, design and construction, while the upriver crew did only location survey, sending their final maps to Haines where the location chief and designer, John McGillvray, had his office.

Our location work was primarily surveying a line up the river for about twelve miles, with design being done right behind our field work. This was all accomplished early on, much of it before my arrival on the scene.

As soon as enough design had been completed, we began putting in construction stakes in preparation for the contractor, who was already setting up shop.

All through the winter the weather was intermittent rain and snow, first about two feet of snow, then rain to pack it down while we slogged around in it, going into the slush to our knees while trying to find the old survey stakes. After the rain comes the freeze from subzero air spilling down the Chilkat river making all the slush holes into rocklike pockets. Then the next foot or so of snow to cover up the pockets and making walking treacherous and slow. It was bad enough under the best of conditions, but worse after the sprained ankle suffered from Indian basketball in rubber boots.

All along the river the road was continually being iced over from the rain fed seepage along the cutslopes. Just getting to work and back was a major effort and more energy was spent there than on productive work.

The constant search under the snow for the stakes of the location survey made it necessary to retrace most of that line before it was possible to do the construction staking. Such conditions make for errors, and we had our share.

The hard freezes were brought on by the extreme cold air of the interior spilling over the mountain passes and sweeping down the Chilkat river in winds of 40 mph or more.

87

Temperatures between zero and 15 below further chilled by the high wind, made it virtually impossible to face toward it for any period of time without frostbite or worse. The wind dried silt of the riverbed would be carried along by the high wind, sometimes in clouds one hundred or more feet high.

The Alaska winter of 1942-3 went down as one of record breaking severity, and we had our share of its benefits. Snag airport, near the Alaska-Yukon border where the highway crosses, recorded a record 82 below at one time, and it was below minus 60 there for more than two consecutive weeks.

Many days it was impossible for us to accomplish anything in the field, so the inside work was kept well up to date. Party chief John Haapala was regularly accused in a friendly way of always being able to find inside work to do on the worst days. Of course, there wasn't really much for him to do in the field anyway, but it didn't help morale for him to drive up to the shivering crew, roll the window down a crack, make a short comment and drive on during those miserable times.

For me, it seemed impossible to keep warm, even though dressed in two sets of underwear, one cotton and one 100% wool, wool pants, wind pants (really rain pants) a sheepskin vest, wool shirt, sweat shirt, parka, and wool mackinaw. Footgear was rubber and leather shoe pacs with felt insoles and several pairs of wool socks to fill up the space. Each evening the insoles would be frozen to the inside of the boots, only removable after subjection to the heat of the oil stove.

Travel back and forth to work was in what we termed a "dog wagon" for the similarity it bore to vehicles used by dog catchers. "Screen sided and covered 1935 Dodge pickup with roll down side curtains" would be a more accurate description.

Sitting on the side benches in the back with our tools at our feet it was just like being in a submarine, except for the lurching, jolting action as we traveled over the slippery, potholed twelve miles of the project. Most miserable of all were the times when our axeman, Hugh Taylor, chose to salvage birch logs for firewood in his rented house. Then the tailgate would be left down and two or more six to eight inch tree trunks laid in the bed amid the rest of the equipment. This way southbound down the river on our homeward way, the north wind could blow into the back and out through the front end of the canopy, chilling tools, logs, and crew alike.

Hugh, the axeman, somewhere in his mid fifties at the time, had the best job of all, affording exercise enough to keep warm while working. Worst off of all was Don Reid, the transitman, required to stand quietly by his instrument all day, kicking his feet against the ground and beating his hands for warmth. Whenever there was lots of brush to cut, plenty of competition took place for the axes, just as an excuse to warm up.

Arriving back at the office after work, cold and miserable, was only compounded while I was living at the rented house with Hector, and when I got back from the trip to Petersburg, I found the living room piled high with wood and the wood cutting operation carried on there as well. That was enough for me, and I accepted the offer by Don and Pozzi to move into the hotel with them as earlier described. Living was better after that, at least during the off duty hours. Wet spruce and subzero temperatures just don't make the most compatible partners for comfortable living.

Shortly after I abandoned Hector, his selective service number (draft) came up, and he went to Juneau to report. This was the only case I know of where any of our engineering crew was drafted.

Survey Crew at 42 mile

Tombstone at 6 mile

CONTRACTORS OPERATIONS

All the while we were stumbling around in the snow and ice out on the road, the management contractor was steadily moving in equipment and building his base of operations in the south part of town, beyond the school. Much of the only area available was low and swampy, so an extensive amount of deep ditching was necessary before it was possible to get an adequate foundation.

The first small contingent of contractors men came in to quickly erect some prefabricated, recycled buildings to serve as quarters and mess hall in preparation for the construction crews to follow. Here, as in the interior, the buildings were from old CCC camps or similar installations, and were set up in only a day or two. Timing was critical, since there were no local facilities capable of providing the necessary food and lodging for a sizeable crew of workmen.

Very early in 1942, while the whole Alaska Highway project was in its formative stages, it became evident to PRA officials that construction equipment, parts, and tools were in such short supply that individual contractors would be unable to carry on work on the scale necessary. As a result, it was decided to use management contractors who could in turn engage individual contractors with their resources to do the construction. The management contractor could then provide the benefits of large support depots and, to a degree coordinate the equipment and supplies needed for the larger job.

This system was also applied to the Haines cutoff when it was added to the work to be done.

The management contractor assigned for our work at Haines was Dowell Construction Co. of Seattle, who had already established a huge depot in Whitehorse and several field camps on the eastern Yukon portion of the Alcan. Thus it was possible for them to divert equipment already in transit from Seattle to Haines instead of Skagway and rapidly build up the Haines headquarters organization.

As soon as quarters were available, the equipment began to arrive, first the tractors for clearing and then two big

91

draglines for ditching and draining the staging and shop area.

Once the site was cleared and drained the facilities mushroomed virtually overnite, with shop, warehouse, and equipment yard rapidly building up amid the mud, snow, and slush. It was soon necessary for PRA to ship in more staff as equipment checkers, timekeepers, and accountants to monitor the operation and assure only a reasonable amount of waste and inefficiency. Time and conditions did not allow preparation of plans and specifications for construction in the normal manner. Rather it was necessary for contractors to take on work without knowing the extent or results expected, and normal bidding would have entailed unacceptable risks for them. Since the Government, in this case the PRA, also did not know precisely what would be required to reach the goal of a road from here to there, work was undertaken on a cost basis, with a fixed-fee profit added. Thus the need for added Public Roads staff to keep track of the hours worked by men and equipment on at least a spot check basis.

Much of the equipment came from CCC, WPA, or similar fleets, already government owned and painted a distinctive dark green to differentiate it from privately owned. This equipment, of course, was paid for at a different cost rate from that of the contractor.

Some contractors tried to ship in equipment which was virtually inoperable, just to pad the cost, but most of this subterfuge was detected at the Port of Embarkation in Seattle. The Northern repair shops really didn't need any more defective and worn out equipment to keep them occupied.

Hiring and keeping adequate personnel was a continuing problem for the contractors, despite high wages and plenty of overtime. Average stay was very short, in the neighborhood of two or three weeks through the winter, despite a minimum stay requirement before return passage would be borne by the government. The steamer Denali of the Alaska line did, at one time, lay offshore in the bay for several days in the bitter cold and windy weather, waiting for the weather to moderate so she could dock at the Barracks. Reputedly, a number of the construction hands refused to go ashore, choosing instead to return to Seattle at their own expense.

92

Once the base shops had been established in Haines, the Dowell Co. chose Colonial Const. Co. of Washington State as the road contractor. The company was owned and managed by Sam Bergstrom, an experienced and well respected superintendent whom we were glad to welcome to the job. Sam chose to construct his camp six miles up the river at a level, well drained site. It, also, was of recycled buildings, with room for about 75 men.

Ruth, Louise, and Marge, Tidehouse, Petersburg

With John Allen at Greenrocks

SOUTH FOR CHRISTMAS

After a few weeks of floundering around in the snow, Christmas was upon us. The prospects of celebrating in Haines weren't too promising, and were further complicated by the fact that only a couple of hundred miles away at Petersburg, my sister Louise was in the midst of her second year of school teaching.

A few miles away in Alaska during wartime is a more than significant obstacle. Limitations on transportation alone, plus the complications of wartime priorities, security, etc. made it hard to imagine how the trip could be made.

I had been planning the trip in the back of my mind to a degree while in Whitehorse, and had bought a Christmas present for Louise, but had already given up and mailed it from Haines. In a big, blue Army barracks bag I had been able to stuff a double sized 4-point Hudson's Bay Blanket, pull the top tight with the Puckering string, tag it, and convince Mr. Kingsbury, the postmaster, to mail it just that way to Petersburg. Louise later said that on arrival at the post office she was sure it was just a bag full of laundry, but all was forgiven when she opened it.

Fortunately for me, the wartime rulebook in Alaska could sometimes be ignored in the face of the need of the citizens, and my case turned out to be one of those times. The Coast Guard was operating a 34' motor cruiser as a cutter up and down the Lynn Canal, one of the converted pleasure craft impressed into wartime service. The skipper, a crusty old Chief Bosun's Mate who frequented the restaurant and bar where we ate, told me if I would be at the dock at 5 AM on Dec. 17 he could take me to Auke Bay, near Juneau.

Unfortunately, on the 16th I was chilling all through the day on the job, and when I turned in for the night things weren't going so well.

Nevertheless, well before the appointed time I was there, fever and all. Off we went for Juneau, chased all the way by a gale force north wind and heavy following sea for the seven hour run. With the wind behind us, icing was not too

95

serious, but I learned later that on the return trip the crew twice had to seek shelter in a quiet inlet and deice the boat.

I am not the best sailor and spent a miserable trip, in and out of the head, altering between seasickness and fever for conscious misery, but once again on land at Auke Bay all was forgiven and forgotten.

Once ashore I found myself ten miles from town, but finally got a ride in, arriving about 5 PM. By that time I was beginning to run down, after the short nite and the long day.

I checked into the Gastineau Hotel, and went into the coffee shop for dinner. As I picked up my room key I made a passing inquiry of the desk clerk if he might know of any passage that might be available southbound. Sure enough, he did. The North Sea, an Alaska Transportation System steamer, was that very moment preparing to cast off for the south, was going to stop in Petersburg, and boarding time was 9 PM. Schedules were never posted, so it was purely accidental that such information was available.

This new information was enough to restore my energies, and I managed to get aboard through the Military Police and other red tape, carrying bedroll, foot locker, and suitcase. After a night in a stateroom the fever seemed to be gone, and twelve hours later by the time we arrived in Petersburg morale and health had been restored and I had already found friends.

During the last hour on the ship I had struck up a conversation with a lady who was also preparing to disembark at Petersburg. She knew all the teachers and everybody else in the town and somehow thought Louise was sort of expecting me. As we went ashore together with her in the lead, she spoke to a tall blond man at dockside, "Gene, you will take care of Louises' brother, won't you? It was Gene Torkilson, a sort of self-appointed guardian of the girls, and when I introduced myself, he said "I thought you'd probably be aboard". "Here, let me take some of your gear."

Gene took me in his 1935 Ford coupe up along the main street of the town and down along the waterfront to a cabin sitting hard against the water at the high tide line. Here lived Louise and her fellow teachers Ruth Wetterborg and Marge Bush. Our arrival quickly roused them out of their Saturday morning doldrums.

The house was a long and narrow building with the kitchen in one end and living room in the center, with two bedrooms on the far end. It had been used as a floating bunkhouse or cookhouse for loggers working in the inlets of the forest. A "Wanagan" in local terms. This label was applied to any mobile or semi mobile building used for personal uses anywhere, either floating as here or land based as with our surveyors in the Yukon.

I met many people, that day, probably the most important being the Physician who prescribed a new drug called Sulfanilamide for what he diagnosed as a strep throat. It was a new and serious disease matched by a new and selectively healing medicine. The fever had ended, leaving a severe sore throat, and felt as if I was swallowing battery acid every time I tried. Under the effects of the magic drug the soreness lasted only about two days more, then was forgotten in the fury of a busy schedule.

After a rather quiet Sunday we went in the evening to the Lutheran church to see the little Norwegians do their Christmas program. Interestingly, the Lutheran Church was the white folks church and the Presbyterian church the one attended by the Native Alaskans. Quite different from Haines with its Mission school. The town, I later discovered, was almost entirely Norwegian in ethnic makeup, which accounted for the predominance of Lutherans. The Presbyterian Church was an outgrowth of the same mission program which was working at Haines.

Each day there we did a lot of visiting, walking in the cold air, but I really couldn't stir up a whole lot of enthusiasm for the great cold outdoors after rolling around in the snow for pay for the past months.

The hot, dry, dusty house was pretty comfortable, and besides, it took three days for my 100% wool Stanfields blue label underwear to dry after we finally got it washed and hung out on the porch. Before that, I just didn't have enough warm clothes to stay outdoors for fun.

Just being around partly family and new and warm friends was enough without a lot of activity.

The local single men had a custom called "Yulebucking", which involved visiting many homes, each of which was to provide a drink to the revelers. After many visits and many drinks, the revelry slowed down and the bucks would take themselves off home to prepare for the next round of celebration and activity.

Norwegian pastries were everywhere. The custom was to exchange them as gifts, and it was tempting, indeed to keep from overdoing when everyone was so encouraging. The people of the village were both generous and curious, and the girls' contention was that many came by just to take a look at Louise's brother.

One day we visited with John and Minnie Allen at their home "Green Rocks" several miles south down the channel. The trip there in Oscar Sandvik's fishing boat "Don Q" was quiet and a lot more pleasant than my time on the Coast Guard cutter. Ruth Wetterborg later married Oscar.

Greens Rocks was a beautiful home situated on a point of rocks immediately beside the steamer channel. John and Minnie Allen were early settlers, and had befriended the girls in a way as to almost be considered foster parents. They had established a large garden and were as self sufficient as it was possible to be in the extremes of the Alaskan climate. It was a truly enjoyable day, and further let me feel that I was spending a family Christmas.

By about Dec. 30 I was beginning to get nervous about passage back to Haines, since in those wartime days no schedules were ever posted for the steamers. The Coast Guard cutter "Commodore" would give only general information, but specific and useful facts were in short supply. The Alaska Transportation System steamer "Northland" was the next scheduled ship northbound, but nobody knew when she would come.

The Sons of Norway, the biggest social group in town, celebrated New years eve with a party and dance for the whole town. This went on until about 2:30 am, after which Gene and I walked the girls back home. There we found the oil heater had plugged up and filled the house with acrid, sooty smoke. Gene took the girls to his place and we dismantled and cleaned the stovepipe. About 5 AM we finished the job and got the place aired out and fit for habitation. After settling in for a nights sleep in the morning hours, we awoke at noon to find a repeat of the same malfunction. This time it was necessary to tear the whole thing down and clean the stove firebox, which was badly sooted up. Soot was everywhere, but many hands enabled us to restore things to a habitable condition with reasonable speed. Fortunately the weather was only slightly below freezing so reasonable comfort could be attained while the work went on. Everything was saturated with the odor of oily smoke, and my clothes retained hints of it months later.

The very next day, Jan. 2, just as we were having breakfast at about 8 AM, a blast from a steamer whistle shocked us into action. The "Northland" had finally arrived on her trip north and it was time to go. All aboard by 11 AM and nine hours later I was standing on the dock at Juneau.

On the ship I had gotten acquainted with another Federal Employee, and we decided to share a room at the Gastineau hotel until I could work out some other arrangements.

Next day it was time to start agitating the captain of the port of embarkation for passage north and to find another place to stay to reduce the financial drain.

Louise's friend and fellow teacher Esther Lindemann had told me to contact her sister and her family, the Taylors, if I was obliged to stay in Juneau, so I located them and moved in, or rather onto the back porch. There I was able to stay while seeing the sights of Juneau and continuing to harass the port authorities for the next week. I even baby sat the two little girls on occasion and generally tried to make myself useful.

Finally, on Jan. 9, after becoming well acquainted with both Juneau and the POE staff, as well as feeling guilty about the length of my stay at the Taylors, I was able to board the Army Transport "David Branch" a troop carrier converted from the Central American fruit trade.

This time I had lone possession of a stateroom for six, and was on board early, taking no chances of being left behind. I couldn't go topside, so was left to sit in the blacked out cabin while the ship prepared to get under way. The only view of the harbor and the action above was the images on the walls projected through the pinhole lenses of the holes in the blackout covers on the windows. Amazing what interest can be generated in the flight of gulls across the walls of a room, all upside down, of course.

As a civilian on an Army boat they weren't sure just what to do with me, but so long as the boat kept moving north I didn't care. That night I shared dinner in the enlisted men's mess with Sergeant Stein, aide to the inspector General for the Alaska Defense Command, who was aboard. We were the only ones in the huge dining room and enjoyed a high level of service from the Filipino messmen The Sergeant was a good traveling companion and we talked at length of what was going on in the whole command. It was the first time I had been able to get a reasonably clear picture of what was going on in the Aleutians, and the ferrying of aircraft to Russia. Col Hodge, an acquaintance from the 18th Engrs of the previous summer in the Yukon was also on board and was a most congenial fellow traveler. He had been assigned as C.O. of the 93rd and was going north to assume command. We later saw him in Haines for the few weeks the regiment was there awaiting transfer.

When I awoke in the morning it was with a start to realize the engines were stopped, usually a sign that the ship is in port. Out the door and to the rail, where I found the launch preparing to go ashore. With the help of one of the Filipino stewards I was able to get all my baggage to the ladder. I staggered down with the foot locker and he tossed the rest over to me.

Once ashore it was necessary to walk from the barracks the mile over to Haines, where I reported in and prepared to go back to working in the snow and cold.

Thus endeth a wartime Christmas caper, well worth all the struggle to attain an island of quiet and reason in the midst of a frantic world.

FAREWELL TO HAINES

The weather continued foul all through March with only an occasional break for clear skies. Out along the river it was always windy, whether rain and snow (south wind) or clear and cold (north wind).

In Haines itself somewhat milder conditions prevailed.

Part of the job was to locate and design a new road from the barracks, now Fort Seward, paralleling the waterfront across to Haines, then across the peninsula to the river to connect with the route to the interior. It really was the beginning of the freight route for the army, bypassing the main street of Haines. Much of this route was through low and swampy ground in the timber, and entailed much difficulty in the snow and water. A new airport also was laid out where the road from town reached the river and turned up toward the interior. The work variety let us keep busy when regular roadwork was impossible due to weather and travel conditions.

Completion of the Army work in the interior caused the construction regiments to be shipped out through Skagway, the 18th Engineers ultimately to Shemya in the farthest reaches of the Aleutian Islands, where they spent two more years up until the end of the war constructing and reconstructing docks and an airfield. They fought more against the elements than the enemy. The 93rd Engineers, a white officered black regiment, also came out through Skagway, but stopped at Ft. Seward en route. They were brought over from Skagway on the David Branch, the same boat which brought me back from Juneau after Christmas. The Branch then returned to Skagway for the 18th, leaving the 93rd at the fort for about a month.

Col. Hodge, the new Commanding Officer of the 93rd was an old acquaintance of the PRA crew from the 18th Engineers of the year before in the interior. He had been executive officer of the regiment. The 93rd did an excellent job of relating to the townspeople while there for the short month. The Chaplain brought his singers and his sermon to the church on at least one occasion, affording both the

101

minister and the choir some relief, and the townspeople entertained the officers in their homes numerous times.

As we of the PRA did earlier, the 93rd sponsored a public dance for the town, once again in the gymnasium. Their resources were somewhat better than ours, with a regimental band to play instead of whoever could be found. The crowd was a real mix of black and white soldiers, and civilians of white and native Alaskan descent and a good time was had by all.

After our management contractor was well set up and the cookhouse going , it became inappropriate for us to continue to eat at the restaurant, so we were ordered to eat at the camp. Food, of course, was much more plentiful and varied, The short walk in the cold morning and evening was only a minor addition to the misery of the weather, but the social life associated with the camp mess hall really couldn't compare with that of the restraurant and bar with its drunks, juke box, and all night poker games.

Rumors continued to fly as the winter progressed, and finally on the last day of March came word that we were to turn the job over to the US Corps of Engineers civilian staff (one civilian and a secretary) and prepare to return to the interior. The Corps had decided to manage the work themselves with the Foley Construction Co. as contractor.

As before, we packed up and waited two days for transport to Skagway. Finally the Sueja III, one of Elliotts converted yachts, came to take us over. In Skagway we once again found overnite lodging in the transient barracks. It was just four weeks less than a year since I had stayed at the Pullen house in the then quiet town of Skagway.

The changes wrought in that year were dramatic. The new buildings and warehouses around the waterfront and the Army takeover of the railroad were only the beginning. In the short time from dusk to dawn there was no chance to look it over, but there was a sense of urgency and activity that bore no resemblance to the pace of the previous year.

Over the hill once more to Whitehorse, with the usual lunch stop at Bennett station. Already the days were growing longer in Whitehorse, and the bright sunshine, although cool, was a welcome change from the gloomy coast. Even where it was thawing, the mud was only a fraction of an inch deep, no longer trying to suck the boots off my feet.

This time we were met at the train and transported to the familiar bull pen barracks. Here the waiting game began again but this time it was "arrive on Saturday, collect our baggage on Sunday, and out on Monday" By Monday afternoon we were 150 miles west of Whitehorse in Elliotts camp at the south end of Kluane Lake. Here, under the watchful eye of Archie Sawyer, we were to spend the coming season constructing a thirty mile section of the Alaska Highway. It could then fulfill its promise of an all weather road to the northland and a supply route to the airfields of Alaska and the Yukon.

Elliott Camp 152 toward Slim's River

Camp 152 looking East, PRA quarters

Christmas Creek Spike Camp

YUKON, 1943
BACK TO KLUANE LAKE

Our train arrived in Whitehorse about 7:00 PM, and we were met and transported to the barracks in the south side of town. There were even friends there to meet us this time, and the bright evening sunshine and dry streets were a welcome change from the Haines weather. It was Saturday, so the town was in a particularly merry mood all around us.

We soon found the warm greeting was not necessarily out of hospitality, but that there were other motives as well.

"How long are you going to be in town?" was the first question.

"I don't know, I haven't even arrived yet".

"Well, if you stay until Monday, be sure to get a liquor permit" was the next comment.

It seems that good Canadian whiskey was available, but limited to one bottle per month, and there was always a crunch on to find a non-drinking friend who would cooperate in working the system.

The changes in Whitehorse between November and April were just as dramatic as the ones of the previous year between April and September.

In the entire area there was 24 hour activity, with contractors men working everywhere and the railroad and river docks and adjacent areas piled high with material and equipment.

In the westerly part of the town the contractors had set up huge yards which gave the overall impression of armies preparing for battle. I guess they were, in fact, though the enemy was time and the elements rather than a human one.

In addition to our road contractors there were those associated with the Canol refinery and pipeline project, managed by the U.S. Corps of engineers. they included the Metcalf, Hamilton, Kansas City Bridge combine and the Foley construction Company. Through the coming season they would build hundreds of miles of pipeline to the oilfields of Norman Wells, Fairbanks, and Skagway, as well as reerect the refinery to be shipped in from Texas.

Our management contractors were Dowell construction Company and E. W. Elliott construction Co., both of Seattle, and Utah Construction Company, obviously from Utah. They were already in the process of assigning companies to specific sections to the east and west.

Bates and Rogers construction company was to do the major bridge work.

Dowell was to manage all the work from about 120 miles west of Whitehorse clear to the eastern edge of the division somewhere near Watson Lake, Elliott had a section of about forty miles in length adjoining Dowell to the west, and Utah was to perform all the work from there to the Alaska border. At least these were the general areas mapped out at the beginning of the season. The camps were numbered in sequence both ways from Whitehorse, with a W or E suffix to indicate which way it was. Distance between base camps varied from thirty to sixty miles. Added smaller ones were established adjacent to major bridge sites where necessary, and "Spike" camps were built away from the base camps to reduce travel time and distance.

After a good sleep and some of Whitey Goodman's good food, we took Sunday to go down to the depot and retrieve the baggage and reorganize for what the following days would bring.

Sure enough, right after Monday breakfast I was called to the construction office where Hugh Stoddardt introduced me to Arch Sawyer, a resident Engineer from Portland, who was to be my boss for the season. Arch was in charge of the only section of road to be constructed by Elliott Const. Co. The headquarters camp was near the village of Silver City, or Kluane, 152 miles west of Whitehorse. There we were assigned a section of about 40 miles, beginning opposite Kloo Lake and extending to beyond Congdon Creek on Kluane Lake. Bill Hebert, from Montana, Spud Canfield, from Idaho, and I were selected to be part of this operation and set out forthwith. We made it to milepost 108, where Ken Sanders was Resident Engineer, and spent the night, going on next day to Elliott's camp.

As mentioned earlier E. W. (Ed) Elliott's organization was unique among the contractors. It was not supervised by one of the large management contractors, but was working independently. It was the same Elliott Company which was operating the fleet of converted yachts, barges, and other craft to furnish transportation support to the whole operation, both Army and PRA.

Through the winter months the contractors had been busy preparing for the construction season of 1943. We found a well built and equipped camp, rapidly being readied for an influx of men and equipment to tackle the assigned sector of work.

Eight long log buildings made up the main part of the camp, with a large shop at the southeast end and a quonset hut anchoring the southwest end of the street. The buildings were constructed with the logs placed vertically against frames, and insulated in the interior against the severe Yukon weather. Roofs were of tar paper, good enough to last for the short duration of their need.

The camp was set back a hundred or so yards from the lakeshore, beside the road, with a broad, open meadow affording a good view of the 70 mile long lake. The unfinished quonset hut, with its arched roof, was to be our quarters. Another was being constructed beside it on the side away from the lake, to be used for the camp commissary. Beyond our quarters the foundation had already been laid for a dispensary. Much lumber and other building material was lying around, but it was easy to visualize what the completed camp would be when ready for the roadwork to begin.

Only final work on the bathroom was yet to be done on our hut, and at first we needed to walk up the camp street to use the bathrooms. Archie Sawyer, being the positive and demanding man he was, soon put us ahead in the priorities of the contractor and dealt with this inconvenience in short order. He knew well how to look after his personal needs and the crew benefitted in the process. It was to be a real treat to have our own showers and a plentiful supply of hot water.

When we arrived in camp about 10 AM, the day was only well started, so we quickly identified our bunks, unloaded our baggage, and with a grunt and grumble from Arch, soon were mobilized for work. Plumb bobs, hand levels, measuring tapes, stakes, and chains were quickly dug out of the equipment cache, and off we went.

107

Elliott was eager to start work as the snow and ice receded, and the big rock bluff which had been such an obstacle to the Army in 1942 would now be blasted away and the new grade built low along the lakeshore rather than high above. The army road had climbed to a point two or three hundred feet above the water to avoid the heavy rock work, and it was now our job to correct it to a better standard.

The high army line over the ridge was already famous as Soldiers Summit, the location of the official dedication and opening of the road in November of the previous year. The summit really wasn't a summit at all, but was a most photogenic and spectacular spot, with the broad, blue lake stretching away from the forested slopes below.

The romance was over for us as soon as we saw what was ahead. A vertical bluff, about 50 feet high, extended along the lakeshore for several hundred feet, and we needed to stake out the slope lines both on the hill, high above and in the water as well. Fortunately, the lake still had its four foot thick cover of ice, so we could take soundings without need for a boat, although setting fill stakes was obviously out of the question in the forty foot deep lake.

Bill Hebert, although still in his early 20's, was an experienced transitman and Arch put him in charge of the field crew.

The first order of business was to find out what we could establish of the original survey and try to get it to relate to the designs which had been provided us. A strong southwest wind was blowing down the Slims River from the frozen fastness of the St. Elias Range, and standing up on the steep slopes was a challenge to even the most surefooted. Snow still covered all the flat areas of the project, so the only place to work was where it was too steep for the snow to stick.

Summer was well on the way, however. The 16 hours of daylight and sunshine would soon reveal the work to be done so the contractor could move in his crews to make use of all the supplies and equipment so laboriously brought in through the winter months.

HOME IN CAMP

All through the winter we had been promised knee-length parkas, but it had been mid-March before they arrived in Haines. Up until then we had used our own personal equipment and managed to survive. It had been difficult to understand the delay, but no doubt a look at the temperature numbers had influenced the delivery. Our zero to -30 coastal temperature couldn't compete with those of the interior, which reached -62, but nobody talked about wind chill in those times. Our wind was always up or down the Chilkat river, 30 to 50 miles per hour, with the sand and snow carried high in the air.

All this is to say we now had the parkas, and for the first days along the lake and Slims river they served us well.

The same tale could be told of the twelve-pound eider-down sleeping bags which we never needed, but were issued well into the spring. We weren't about to allow either item to escape now that we had them, since they might yet become useful.

Our camp, was a day's drive from Whitehorse, and soon became a popular overnite stop. It was better appointed than many, and both Army and civilian travelers soon found the food was the best along the road. Elliotts sea transport services seemed to have resulted in some spinoff so far as the shipment of food was concerned, and we were the beneficiaries.

When I say good food, perhaps a description of the array of table goodies which confronted a crewman as he came to breakfast will best picture it: Orange, tomato, or other juice, served from the can, no limit, eggs, fried three ways, scrambled or boiled, toast, french toast or pancakes, bacon, ham, or sausage, two or three kinds of jam or jelly, syrup, butter, and two or three kinds of canned fruit to top it all off. Plenty of coffee, but no fresh milk. This was before the day of reconstituted milk, and canned milk was the staple for coffee drinkers. No limit on the quantities available to these hungry workers, and they groaned as they finished and got up to prepare their own lunches from the heavily laden table at the other end of the room.

Lunch could be prepared from several kinds of lunch meat, cheeses, canned sardines, kippers, or similar wares, along with plenty of fresh fruit, pickles and other garnishes. No limit again, just don't take more than you can eat. No fresh lettuce, but not many other shortages.

Nothing was spared for the evening meal. At least two kinds of meat, preferably steak and ham, with pork chops also a frequent offering. Not much fish or chicken. Turkey on Sunday but red meat for those who wanted it. Usually plenty of potatoes, mashed, boiled or baked, and gravy to cover. Sweet potatoes not too popular, and even liver for those who cared for it. At least two kinds of canned vegetables, and two or three desserts, either fruit or baked goods. Salads as the fresh goods allowed, more cabbage than lettuce. All in all plenty of anything a working man could think of, but the cool weather and active schedule didn't show much weight gain.

There was, indeed a war on, but a look at the table caused it to be forgotten in the midst of such a plenteous feast. The canned goods were an ever present source of amazement to the Canadians, who were more used to lighter weight and lower cost.

Nearly every noon would find army transport trucks of the 340th Engineers lined up in front of camp, seeking relief from Army chow lines in a sit down dinner in the big dining hall. Actually, it was all at Federal expense, so no great issue was ever made of the cost, and even the highest ranking officers, including the Canadians, were quick to join in the act. Forget being an example to the men when good food was available.

At each meal, we and the contractors crew would file in and find our places and the head waiter would then seat the visitors in order of arrival. No serious protocols, although Arch insisted that the second table from the front be unofficially designated for our engineering crew.

The makeup of the construction and cookhouse crews was a lesson in variety. In general, the contractors equipment operators were experienced and competent, but the semi-skilled and unskilled laborers were notable for a variety of backgrounds. The camp maintenance people, known as bull-cooks, and the waiters and laborers all carried the same sta-

110

tus and pay scale. They were paid 85 cents per hour and were assigned duties in line with their physical capabilities rather than by any particular skill they may have possessed. Our head waiter, Karl, the only name I ever knew him by, was a wispy old Scandinavian barber from Minnesota. He took his job very seriously, assuring that mess hall discipline and order were always strictly observed. Each meal he would stand beside the door as the hungry men streamed in, separating the regulars from the transients. He would wave the visitors aside until the crewmen were all in their places and seated, then direct them to any vacant seats.

His lack of concern for name or rank is probably best illustrated by an occasion regarding Lt.Col. Campbell, sector commander in charge of the Army policy in our area, everything west of Whitehorse and east of Alaska. One evening the Colonel showed up with another American officer and a Canadian Major in the middle of the suppertime rush, seeking seats for his party at one of the heavily laden tables. When Karl spotted the three uniformed men he held them aside with his left arm as the others quickly filed by, then turned to the rotund little Colonel and said:

"Wait here and I'll see what I can do for you".

He then walked down the center aisle between the already eating men, seeking three places reasonably close together. Finally, from halfway down the room, he turned, held up his hand and called loudly above the din:

"O.K. Shorty, I can fix you up now". Col. Campbell, always equal to the occasion, only smiled as he shepherded his guests down the aisle between the amused workers. For his part, Karl, totally oblivious to this complete disregard of protocol, busily went about the business of taking care of his boys.

Work Starting below Soldiers Summit

Completed Road below Soldiers Summit, Kluane Lake

WORK TO BE DONE

Elliott's work consisted of four major work areas, virtually all on new location and well away from the Army road. The section near Kloo lake and on the Christmas Creek Summit were both far enough from the main camp to require construction of spike camps. These each consisted of a cookhouse of sawn lumber surrounded by a dozen or so tent frames for the crew. Sanitary facilities consisted of outdoor washstands and a large, multipassenger outhouse well away from the living quarters. The long workdays and even longer daylight hours made any other facilities unnecessary for the men, and the main shop took care of all repairs and paper work.

The other two sections of work were the construction of the bridge across Slim's river and the grading of its adjacent fills and the Soldiers summit rock cut and beyond along the lake . These were close enough and convenient enough to be worked directly out of the main camp.

As surveyors, engineers, or whatever our title might be, we never moved into a spike camp, but stayed in our quonset hut for the entire time.

The contractor was eager to start work on the bridge at the earliest possible time, so it was necessary for us to stake it prior to doing any work in preparation for grading in the still frozen soil.

The new bridge location was a mile or more downstream from the Army bridge, constructed the previous year, and would require long approach fills across the alluvial river flat on both sides. All piling and deck material were of native timber, the piling from the forest south of camp and the deck and other lumber sawed from local timber in a sawmill left by the army from 1942.

Much effort was expended and mud experienced to get all the line to fit across the Slim's River, where the glacial silt from the summer flows had formed its mile-wide plain. Each day it would thaw a few inches, leaving soft mud atop the rock-hard ice beneath. Driving stakes was nearly impossible and the instruments could not maintain their stability

113

in the thawing ground. Finally we managed to complete the stakeout and release the site by early April well prior to the breakup of the river. The contractor achieved his goal of getting his equipment in place while the ground was still frozen and work began on the twelve hundred foot long bridge. Drilling and blasting a hole for each pile through the four foot layer of frozen sediment became the order of the day for a few weeks until warm weather gradually solved the problem.

By May 1 we were able to move our engineering work toward Christmas Creek and Kloo Lake to prepare for major grading. All this time the Army road was steadily deteriorating from the thawing and traffic was having more and more difficulty. Finally, just as we were getting on with our stakeout of the new alinement, spring weather began to heal the road and traffic became less and less impeded by the muddy conditions.

Our winter crews had already flagged most of the clearing limits throughout the project, and the contractors clearing operation stayed well ahead of our staking. It was still impossible to excavate in the frozen ground. No burning of clearing debris was done. The timber was either cut or pushed down, and the resulting debris piled in windrows well back from the construction area. This sometimes caused problems for the survey crews in tying the designed line to the location of the previous year, but was still much the most effective way of clearing the area.

Time for reconstruction

TIME OFF TO BE SICK

By the start of May work had been under way for over a month on the dispensary/infirmary behind our quonset hut, but it was not yet staffed when I began to have an unexplained swelling on the left side of my neck. After a couple of days of misery and increased swelling, it was possible to see an army doctor attached to the 340th engineers transportation group. His hot water bottle remedy didn't do a thing for it, however, so off to Whitehorse after work one evening. I arrived about 5 AM at the bullpen, and after three hours sleep made my presence known to the front office and went over to the hospital. There Dr. Doyle took a look and told me to keep the heat on and come back in a day or two.

Being in town in the good weather and long days of summer with a little idle time was a new experience. There was much activity in progress and there were many friends to visit. Fred Johnson, my old chief from 1942, was in the process of making up his crew to go Destruction Bay, just west of our project on a Utah Construction Co. job. Chuck Ellis from Lednickys crew was also in town for a few days. In fact there were any number of old friends coming and going as the construction season began to unfold. I found that we had been among the earliest to go out into the field and that things were just beginning to take shape, particularly far to the west beyond Kluane Lake and Burwash Landing.

The personnel people became more and more nervous after seeing me around for a few days ambulatory, yet not able to do any productive work, so after a week of daily checks with Dr. Doyle, he finally sent me back to camp. I managed to get a ride out of town on one of Dowells freight trucks as far as Camp 2-W for the night, then on to 152 mile next day with another driver. . .

One day on the job and the swelling went up overnite worse than ever. Fortunately, I got a ride to town in an Army ambulance this time, arriving in time for Dr. Doyle and a new doctor, Dr. Hart, to give me some medication. Worse than ever next morning, I was given a bed in the hospital

115

where they could watch me get lumpier and lumpier as the days passed.

The hospital, operated by the Public Health Service, took up two of the long, narrow wings of the building complex.

It was staffed by two doctors, a dentist, four or five Canadian nurses and a sanitarian. All seemed highly professional and competent, and the whole operation was smoothly run.

All medical and medically related matters and camp sanitation in the whole division, from Watson Lake to Alaska were the responsibility of this small staff. Contractors men, US Civilian employees of all agencies, and Army personnel were all treated, although the exact status of the Army was never really clear to me.

For over a month it was in and out of the hospital as the infection waxed and waned. The doctors were continually seeking reasons for the persistence of the infection (their word), but never were able to find the answer.

Other than the medium discomfort, of a sore neck, I was ambulatory, and spent much time making beds, carrying trays, and otherwise trying to make myself useful and inconspicuous. The nurses seemed able to find something for me to do much of the time when asked, but were always apologetic about requesting help. It was a new kind of supervision for me, and easy to adjust to.

One of the patients, and ex County Extension Agent from Louisiana, Russell White, had come in to the hospital during my first stay. He had been injured pulling the cable off the winch on his tractor when the clutch had slipped into gear, tightening the cable over his left hand severely crushing it and breaking fifteen or more bones. I well remember hearing his agonizing groans as the doctors sought to set the bones and stitch him up in the early hours one morning.

For several days he was in great agony, but after a week the hand rapidly began to heal.

Here was a new job for me.

As the wounds healed, the skin was developing hard, dry scar tissue and internal adhesions were progressively stiffening his hand.

The job of rubbing oil on the hand and seeking to make it flexible fell to me as captive and cheap labor.

116

In doing the therapy I was instructed to first soften the skin by massage, then, from time to time when he was well relaxed, to apply force to open up the fingers from their clenched position. Needless to say, it was painful to Russell, and the first time I stretched the adhesions he became upset, if not angry. The doctors and nurses kept him convinced I had only his best interests at heart, and we managed to maintain our mutual peace and friendship through it all.

The 24 hour daylight made it difficult to enforce lights out and quiet in the wards, particularly with garrulous patients. This was of great concern to the nurses, and they were constantly trying to enforce the discipline of quiet. It is difficult for a bunch of construction men to keep still when they all have stories to tell and each tries to top the rest. All the confrontation was in good spirits, and the nurses finally gave up in frustration once we promised to keep the level of noise fairly low. Except for me, everybody was injured, not sick, and once free of pain was ready to visit and not to be denied.

The social life around the headquarters was fairly active. There were at least a dozen single women who had been brought in from the states for support help. They were all regular civil service employees, though some quite young. Added to these were the three single nurses. All this female presence afforded a certain opportunity for a reasonable degree of social life. It was a new exposure to me after being strictly in the field in a man's world for over a year except for the time at Haines.

The perspectives of the field personnel and headquarters were somewhat different and I came to resent somewhat the cavalier treatment accorded the field men as they passed through for reassignment. After working long hours almost continuously under difficult conditions of both work and housing for months at a time, the men would come through on an official transfer, only on occasion to be hassled by the headquarters clerks for loitering in the hallway or otherwise appearing to be idle and unoccupied. Div. Engr. Frank Andrews and Const. Engr. Hugh Stoddardt, to whom we were really responsible, understood well, and had no problem, but it seemed the administrative underlings were somewhat insensitive to the isolation felt by the men. After being part

117

Soft Spots

Christmas Creek Cutoff

Closing the Gap, Slim's River Br.

of the headquarters for over a month, I felt this concern even more strongly than before. It seemed the assumption by the office force was that only they had a proper sense of mission, yet they were working regular hours in very normal living conditions. I would never begrudge them the opportunity to enjoy a normal living pattern, but a little more empathy toward the men out there actually building the road would have been appreciated.

After about three weeks of treatment in the hospital, Dr Doyle one morning walked into the ward, took one look at my neck, and called for me to come into the treatment room. There they stuck a needle in to desensitize me, then sliced the lump open to drain. No wonder it hurt with all that stuff in there.

About a week more and then back to camp I went, glad to escape to my normal world.

Summer had arrived while I was gone. Much of the original staking had been completed, and by July 1 both ends of the job had significant amounts of grading done, Our work now consisted of routine staking and keeping up with the contractors needs.

More and more the management of the contract became a priority.

I found equipment checkers had been added to our staff, as well as more surveyors, and we had overflowed our quonset hut and into one of the contractors barracks.

Six Canadian College Students, mostly from Univ. of Sask. had come for the summer. They were a welcome help and enabled us to field two crews to better provide for control of the work.

Arch in his diplomatic way kept the students all completely intimidated by never speaking, to them or acknowledging their existence in any way. but that was his normal way of relating. He never spoke to or respected me, either, until he trapped me into an argument and I respectfully stood my ground despite a bit of his verbal abuse. After that he was always civil and friendly, and even became an advocate at times.

The checkers were necessary to assure that all equipment reported as working was, indeed, doing so, and that only repairable items were being repaired.

Like many others, our contractor had brought some unnecessary and/or disabled equipment to the project, and the temptation was great to charge it off as working. Our equipment expert, W. D. Fernley, was highly competent and knowledgeable, as well as a good diplomat, and conflicts were kept to a minimum. We heard horror stories from other locations, so considered ourselves fortunate.

During the month I had been away, the infirmary had been completed and staffed with my old friends Dr. Hart and nurses Kay Young and Charlotte Storey, assigned from the Whitehorse hospital.

About a week after I returned, once again I got a high fever and aches and pains Dr. Hart ordered me to bed. Not in the hospital this time, but in our quonset hut, where my bed was only about thirty feet from the hospital door.

Doctor Hart suspected pneumonia and asked what medication I had received in Whitehorse. Not knowing and not having any way of finding out, he decided to use sulfa, a new drug, hoping it hadn't been used before and an immunity developed. Apparently it was a good diagnosis, for five days later I was back to work again.

To Archie Sawyer's credit, he never charged me for leave time, and justified it by insisting I never left my official quarters.

Kay Young, Dr. Hart, Charlotte Storey. Dispensary, Camp 152

121

Clem swats a big one

Elliott Camp 240 Mile, Badluck Creek No. 2

FINISHING UP AND WINDING DOWN

At the peak of the construction season we began to feel the effects of Army orders issued in the spring which had drastically changed our 1943 mission. After most of the final design had been completed by people working in the States, the Army policy was changed. Instead of an all weather, two lane road constructed to a consistent standard, they decided to follow the location of the original pioneer road as much as possible, not worrying much about sharp curves and steep grades. We were to only deviate when it was so bad as to be totally impractical for trucks to travel.

Fortunately for us, a large portion of the original road on our section was not feasible for use, and our fast start in the spring on grading and bridge construction resulted in our constructing close to the designed alinement through much of the project.

To assure compliance with Army policy, a contingent of three civilian representatives of the U.S. Corps of Engineers was detailed to our camp. In charge was Cliff Thompson, a highway engineer from Montana. He was a highly practical and knowledgeable engineer, and he and Archie seemed to have a good understanding, considering the restraints of the official relationship.

As I returned to work we were connecting up the major sections of work earlier discussed, and wherever the Army road could be renovated, restored, or rejuvenated, we did so. More and more at my level it seemed we were putting out a lot of effort to salvage something better abandoned, and at no significant saving in either time or money.

In several places we had completed right of way clearing and staking for long sections of our original designed line when we were instructed to stop. Instead of completing, we ran line down the army road and staked it for widening and surfacing only.

Late in July, transitman Slim Jankowski, a forester from Minnesota and Univ. of Calif., took on a job of property surveying for Jack Hayden, owner of land at the site of the ghost town of Silver City or Kluane. Jack claimed 40 acres and showed us a square wood post on the sidehill which he claimed to be his northwest corner.

Simple enough. One Sunday we set up over it and measured out a quarter of a mile south, east, north and west to the point of beginning, more or less. For $25 and use of Jack's launch any time, it was not too bad a morning's work. Later on in the summer the U.S Geological Survey survey in establishing a control network for mapping purposes, tied in our survey to theirs. Our credibility was established, and made part of the permanent maps. We never put our names on anything, just drove stakes in the ground with a little writing on them.

In 1942, a similar thing happened another hundred miles north at Grafe creek and my name went on the map as a result. Getting there first is what really counts.

We kept hearing rumors of contractors being bogged down far to the northwest, particularly beyond the Donjek and White rivers. The pioneer road in those areas of deep permafrost where we had surveyed in 1942 was completed late in November. This had not allowed time for the civilian followup to place gravel before freezeup, and the bottom went out with the spring thaw. With alert maintenance the major bridges had been saved. The ever deepening mud in the narrow roadway ultimately became only a ditch, with tractors pulling the trucks through in some areas.

Fortunately, all was not just work.

Cliff Thompson, the Corps of Engineers rep in camp, had access to an army bridge pontoon and a 22 hp motor which had been used to power an Army ferry somewhere. One Sunday he invited Jim Holderman from our crew and me along for a ride on the lake. Some ride. We went about halfway down the lake, then about 20 miles up into the Big Arm, a long inlet on the north side of the lake. Cliff only caught three fish, so it was a lost cause to him, but it was a highlight to me. We were gone about ten hours and traveled about 10 mph. The big pontoon, with its straight sides really wasn't very seaworthy, and coming back to camp in the dark in the face of a south wind we managed to end up wet and cold. Jim and I each had carried our lunches but they didn't go far for the appetites of six hungry men. Fortunately it only got dark for about two hours before we got back

124

at 1:15 AM. Monday was not a good day. When we thought of the 3 gallons a week gasoline rationing going on in the States, it was with a twinge of conscience for burning so much on a boat ride, but it didn't last long.

Back to work. We finally connected up with the crew to the east at Milepost 121, Jarvis creek. At that point both contractors were strictly improving the pioneer road, and a new bridge of native timber was being built over the stream adjacent to the existing one.

Despite all the restrictions on construction, we constantly sought to establish the relationship between the existing road and the 1942 survey. This would enable later workers to use the design as developed.

Friday, August 13, my birthday. Everybody wore neckties for me. Humbling and flattering.

All the time we were working, the 340th Engineers, now a transportation regiment, was busily hauling freight through the project. They no longer used the 2 1/2 ton 6x6 Studebaker trucks of the previous year. Now the trucks were higher and without duals on their tandem rear axles. Neither were they painted the traditional army green, but a sand color, almost pink. We were told the trucks were originally scheduled to go to the desert of North Africa, but that events there changed their mission. The fortunes of war do strange things to the best laid plans.

Late August found us working all over the project as Elliott rapidly completed work on the originally assigned section. More rumors of long delays and failing schedules up the road kept us on edge as fall approached, and, sure enough, in Mid-September our five man crew left the camp at 152 mile for a 90 mile trip to 240 mile, a new camp beyond the Donjek River. Here Elliott was to take on another fifteen miles of work, extending from the Donjek river westerly toward the White.

The camp was located just west of Bad Luck Creek, about a quarter of a mile upstream from where our survey crew had established our Starvation camp in 1942. Here the army road, running north from its crossing of the Donjek, far upstream of our line, once more joined and adopted our 1942 location survey alignment.

Camp construction had been started by the original con-

125

tractor, and it was well along when we and Elliott moved in. It was designed along the lines of a regular spike camp, only somewhat more self contained. A large shop and two large quonset huts were included in this one, luxuries not normal to such camps. Our quarters were initially in a partially completed tent frame, 14 x 16 feet with an oil barrel stove. Through a little creative stealing we were soon able to make it reasonably comfortable for the increasingly cold weather ahead.

We found both the project engineering and construction were in deep trouble, considering the late September date. One of the Utah companies had gotten off to a late start, then suffered from mismanagement, breakdowns, and lack of parts. They had generally been unable to accomplish anything on the half of their project west of the Donjek River. To the east they had made reasonable progress, almost entirely by rebuilding the Army road. At that point it descended the hill onto the river flats to cross the several bridges of the braided channel. The bridges had been saved from going out during the breakup by stationing a dragline there to keep debris and ice floes from carrying them away.

Glen Nelson, the Resident Engineer, was primarily a locator and designer, and a good one, but disliked construction. He was very sincere in his remarks when we arrived: "I'm sure glad to see you guys. At last somebody who knows what to do".

He seemed rather defeated by the whole thing, and hadn't been helped by receipt of a "Dear John" letter from his wife at the peak of the season.

Glen brought his design to us from his Utah camp at the Donjek River and we laid them out on the dining hall tables where he could show us what he had in mind.

The army crossing was about two miles upstream from where we had run our 1942 line to locate the bridge at the mouth of the canyon. From that crossing to our present camp it pretty well followed our old horse trail.

It was necessary for us to land running, staking out the widening of the clearing, and setting controls for the contractor to improve and widen the road. This would be done by hauling from the river bars, filling as we went to stay atop the permafrost. The original road had been built in a simi-

126

lar way through the dense spruce forest, using the tree trunks to form a foundation prior to filling. The only real grading we did on the section between camp and river was at the bridge approach. There a big sidehill cut was made in the frozen ground in order to have a proper approach to the bridge. Once that was done, the soil gradually flowed down into the road as the cut face thawed, causing a constant maintenance problem in the summer.

From our new camp to the west, the Army had generally followed our 1942 location, and we were able to use some of the design provided.

As we got into providing controls for the contractor and dialogue with Glen, it became more and more evident he really meant it when he said he wanted us to take charge of the west section, despite his ultimate responsibility for it. Here we were, neither paid or qualified to take on field design while a job was already under contract. Absent information to the contrary, full speed ahead, and we never dared look back. If it had been anything but a cost plus contract it would have scared everybody a lot worse.

Arch Sawyer, too, had pretty much left things up to us, so we proceeded to free locate along the road, assisted by the contractors grade foreman. Fortunately, he was an experienced County Engineer from Minnesota and was able to direct the contractors operation once we all agreed on how to go.

In the midst of all this, Commissioner of Public Roads Thomas H. McDonald was scheduled to come through about Sept. 19 or 20 to see what could be done further north, where things were steadily getting more and more desperate. Upon instruction we marked out some mileposts for him, then never heard any more. We did hear he stayed in our quarters at 152. If he passed by us at work, we never knew it.

Finally, on Sept. 27, we were able to connect our project survey with the next project to the west at mile 250. From there on Resident Engineer Del Earley had had good success and the road had been pretty well completed clear to the White River, There the new permanent bridge was under construction. We were now able to drive up the road and take a look at what had been done.

It was a real treat to go up the road along Lake Creek,

Pioneering in the big ditch

Jack Obermeyer and Stan Brown above the Donjek

Main Channel, Donjek River Br.

Army road beyond the Donjek

across Grafe creek, where a bridge was under construction, and on past Pickhandle lake to the White River crossing. Nearly all the road had been built by the Army on our location, since the 29th Engineers had worked so closely with us in 1942. Driving over the road was a far cry from the slogging through the permafrost and over the niggerhead swamps of the previous year.

Makeup of the crew was constantly changing as the season progressed, with all the summer student help departing. Slim, Jim, and I were the only ones there from start to finish.

Harold Slattery, a planning survey engineer from New York was brought out to be our supervisor, since he carried a good pedigree and was on the payroll. When we showed him what we were doing and got him in the field, we found him completely at sea as to what was going on. He went back to town after a couple of days, and we went ahead on our own. Not his fault, he was just completely out of his element.

The crew movement was to some degree an advantage, since old friends came and went in the procession. Jack Obermeyer and Stan Brown showed up for a few days, and when they found out we were living right beneath our camp meat hunting grounds from the previous year, persuaded me to guide them on a hunt.

I was easy to persuade, and early one Sunday morning we took the old trail up Starvation creek to the lake. As we turned east at the outlet and up the long grassy slope we spotted a huge bull moose knee deep in the lake, grazing on the water plants. Each time he raised his head to swallow, we could see the sun reflected off his antlers. Even from our vantage point several hundred yards away, he looked huge. Sheep were our goal, though, and we continued on to the top of the mountain. Luck was with us. Jack and Stan each bagged a sheep. One large ram and a mature ewe. Now for the fun. After dressing out the kill, each made up a pack by interlocking front and rear legs and started off down the hill. I followed along behind with head, guns and packboard. In all we saw 2 wolves and 17 sheep. I was pleasantly surprised to find game since we had considered last year that we had spooked all the game away The following week they tried again, but even our pet moose had left the country.

The Canadian government in 1942 had authorized the harvest of game for camp meat, but, even though the sheep were served up to the crew, it seemed to me to be stretching the intent of the permission.

Finding his carpenters needed work, Mr. Johnson, Elliott's superintendent, took it upon himself to build a house over at the east end of the camp where it was unobserved until nearly complete. On Archie's third weekly visit it finally came to his attention. The bright, freshly sawed lumber stood out in sharp contrast to the tents and quonset huts of the rest of the camp. The only other such building was the outhouse down below the road near the power plant.

"What's that?" asked Archie when he spied the shiny new building.

"Oh, I understand that's for the use of the general superintendent when he comes to visit".

"Who the hell does he think he is, we're not paying any money for him to have a vacation home".

"Don't know, Arch, that's what we've been told."

"Well, if the government's going to pay for it, we might as well enjoy it."

No argument from us. It was getting cold in the tent, even if the bullcook did keep the fire going for us. Temperatures were already in the low teens as we moved into October, and nobody hesitated when Arch told us to move in.

The first night in the house, Arch showed up and spent it with us there, just to gloat a little, help us enjoy our good fortune, and get a few strokes about what a good deal he had found for us. Small enough price for us to pay for an inside toilet. The eightholer down by the power plant had only the exhaust for a heater, not quite enough to do the job in the cold weather.

With the end of September came the realization that it was getting wintry. First snow at Kluane came on Sept. 20, just five days later than the previous year, and a definite cooling was immediately apparent.

Our initial engineering work was completed, enabling the contractor to work throughout either one if the jobs. Cleaning up and finishing required our attention whenever

131

called for, but the pressure was off. This gave time to devote to the permanent surveying and referencing the line.

Work involved tying together the 1942 survey and the as-constructed road, reconciling them into one set of data. This was sometimes troublesome, since haste makes for errors and there was plenty of both. Big discrepancies were found when the surveys were connected and computed. A few, but not all of the errors were resolved to reasonable satisfaction.

It was simple to tie to the new USGS metwork which had been run up the valley. Only the survey points on the ground were available, so distances and bearings to them were adequate. Somebody, somewhere, sometime probably tried to make sense out of it. Good luck, the tracks were pretty faint.

Jim Holderman and I took one last trip up the line to mile 280, beyond the White river. Things were getting pretty desperate up there toward Alaska. It was now almost mid-October and some of the contractors were just gaining access to their work areas. They had been bogged down digging out mud and backfilling with gravel for most of the season.

The White River bridge had been under construction since late winter, and when we were there they were pouring the piers in weather approaching zero. Big houses over the whole operation just to keep the concrete from freezing before it set. The bridge was right on the line which we had located, the only place to cross within miles, right at the mouth of the canyon.

We found Cliff Polk, from Haines days, now Alaska Division Engineer, and J.B. Reher, Location Engineer, both up at 280 mile commiserating on the state of things. It was not a pretty picture, but time and the cool weather would soon provide a solution for the winter, even if the contractors were unable to complete before freezeup.

We never went back up north again, but later were given to understand the job was completed, covering the last miles by launching a massive hauling operation. As a result the next season was not a repeat of 1943. We heard down the line that a victory of sorts was declared on October 13.

Just as we were winding up our work, and with the

rumor mill grinding out its Nov. 1 threatened deadline date for completion and return home, my left eye became inflamed, just like pink eye. We were still going back and forth between projects and didn't bother to have it checked out at the camp infirmary. Finally on one of the Sunday trips back to 152 mile the doctor took one look and brought things to a halt. He was headed in to Whitehorse in an ambulance and I was told to go in with him, taking along all personal gear.

Good bye camp and back to town.

Doctors Doyle, Hart, and Spencer, and nurses Cody and Storey all treated me like a preferred and regular customer. Hard to tell about the former, but no question about the regularity.

After a few minutes with the Doctors, Charlotte Storey came and said: "We have your old bed ready". Some way to enter the hospital.

The doctors were not by any means confident of a proper diagnosis except to call it an "iritis", which means something wrong with the iris, and they freely admitted it. They said they were going to sort of experiment, and I really didn't have much choice but to agree.

Tuesday morning Dr. Spencer, the dentist, walked into the ward and invited me to his treatment chair. One look and consensus was arrived at that it just might be an infected wisdom tooth. Out it came and back to the ward for me to wait it out.

Nothing apparently wrong with that tooth, just badly located, but the rest took their turns anyway. Treatment cost and quality of care were without peer, but the results were only a sore jaw and not a well eye.

Time for the next stage. As explained to me, the body uses fever to kill infection, therefore, if we can get a good fever going and hold it long enough, maybe the eye problem will go away. No comment from me. I'm both the customer and the victim.

Right after dinner the head nurse. Bea Hawkinson, came in with a big needle full of typhoid fever serum and shot it into the vein in my right arm. I was advised to expect some chilling and then a buildup of fever, which, hopefully would go high enough and last long enough to do the job.

133

Sure enough, in a couple of hours I was shaking so badly it rattled the bed, even with three or four hotpads and hot water bottles in critical places. About four hours of that and the fever did, indeed, go up, topping out at 104 and holding. Over the next 40 hours it gradually tapered off and the doctors thought they would soon detect some clearing of the clouded iris.

One more day and no improvement, so another dose of serum. This time the whole cycle was completed by noon the day after the shot, so no therapy occurred. Fever was supposed to stay up a minimum of three days to really be effective. By this time large areas of skin were peeling off both hands and feet. Some sort of low grade fever blisters. Now for heavy applications of Whitefields ointment to help out.

That only served to make it easier to strip off the skin.

The deadline date of November 1 had come and gone. All during the hospitalization I was enjoying a steady stream of visitors, passing through headed south and home by rail, boat, truck, or plane.

All at once I began to hear the word "evacuate" as they discussed my fate. This seemed to mean "Get him out of here to where special care and skill are available."

The final word came at last in the form of a visit from Frank Andrews, Division Engineer, who took the time to come into the hospital and tell me what was up. This was typical of him, a real gentleman who cared about his staff in an extraordinary way, and thereby earned their respect and coperation.

"Well, Grafe, things are winding up here at a pretty fast pace, and, in fact, most of the field men have already gone home," he said. "The doctors here tell me they really aren't satisfied with what they can do for you, so we plan to fly you out, back home to Portland, where they are sure you can find better care." "We're working on your transportation right now, and you should be prepared to leave in a day or two."

This sort of approach didn't leave much room for argument, so I thanked him and prepared to follow his instructions. It was really no time to discuss responsibility for health care, even if I had thought about it. Too much time had al-

134

ready been spent in the hospital and the opportunity to get out looked good to me.

That very day there were papers to fill out and arrangements to be made to ship out everything but hand baggage needed for the flight home.

Nov. 20 was the big day. Just one year to the day since the road had been officially opened and dedicated at Soldiers Summit. Our CPA Lockheed Lodestar took off at 12:40 and with only one stop at Watson Lake, I ended up in Ft. St. John for the night. Right in the middle of the wheat country, and the lakes weren't even frozen yet. Fresh milk and bad water were the two most impressive things about Ft. St. John, unless it could be the all night party downstairs.

I was weak and one-eyed after three weeks of all that good therapy and bed rest, but so long as we were headed south it was ignored. Sure enough, south we went again with a stop at Prince George. There Gordon Warren, Pan-Am radio operator from Burwash was working in the terminal, and the long stopover gave me a chance to visit him.

On to Vancouver and a night in the Hotel Vancouver. Quite a change from the hospital and barracks bullpen, but easy to make the cultural adjustment.

Train to Seattle, then on to Portland to complete the loop started 20 months earlier.

My sister Louise was staying in Oregon City, preparing for a Dec. 12 wedding, and I was able to stay with her future in-laws, the Taylors while quitting the job and healing the eye.

Up to the PRA office, where I had hired out in April of 1942, only this time to resign, walk out unemployed and infected, and go look for my own medical help.

The Taylor family Optometrist, Dr. Friedman, sent me to Dr. Gaston, an Opthamologist who had returned to practice for the war effort. He inspected the problem, dilated it, inspected it some more, and told me to come back after five days.

This gave time to go home to Idanha for Thanksgiving and to meet the new stepmother, brothers, and sisters, twelve months after we had become relatives.

Back to Portland, where the doctor was noncommittal and invited me to come back in five more days. This time he gave me a shot in the arm which seemed, after five more days, to do some good.

Two more visits to the doctor and he finally released me, cured.

The shots were concentrated vitamin A, not medication at all. The problem, as he diagnosed it, was neither a disease nor infection, but a vitamin deficiency.

Somehow, despite all the best of camp food that could be provided, growing up on the farm and eating from the garden must have made my system somehow dependent on fresh vegetables in a way which could never have been anticipated. Just not enough fresh carrots in the Yukon, I guess.

After effects of the eye caper were confined to recovery from six weeks of dilation and minor astigmatism from a scarred retina. The former took three or four years to reduce the size of the pupil to match the other one, and the latter gradually diminished until it became is unnoticeable.

More interesting was the residual effect of the fever therapy.

Two or three times a year over the next ten or twelve years, the heavy chills and fever of those days were repeated, running their course in about 24 hours. It bore all the symptoms of malaria and was so identified by the US Navy, despite my protestations.

With the curing of the eye, the association with the Alaska Highway ceased for a time, only to emerge again thirty years later, four thousand miles away in Washington D.C.

EPILOGUE

The welcome home was reinforced by an immediate change in draft classification from 2B to 1A, and it was time to prepare to participate in the war effort in a whole different way.

With a brother and two stepbrothers already in the Navy, it didn't take much time to make the decision to follow in their still warm footsteps.

After Louise's wedding things moved rapidly, and I soon found myself sworn into the Worlds Greatest Canoe Club and aboard the train for Farragut Naval Training Station on the shores of Lake Pend Orielle in far north Idaho. A long ways from the ocean, in fact a lot more like the Yukon than anywhere else, and the six weeks of Boot Camp passed quickly.

At the end of the six weeks, testing showed the training staff that I was supposed to undergo more training, this time as an Electronics Technicians Mate, learning all about a new concept called Radio Direction and Ranging (RADAR). Training was to begin in a National Guard Armory in Michigan City, Indiana. There three hundred of us were bunked three high in the big drill room/gymnasium, and our group, last to arrive, was assigned to the top bunks. Here I could reach over and place my clothes in the convenient basketball hoop while sitting on my bunk at bedtime. Really high living, (or sleeping).

Michigan City is situated just east of Gary, right beside the tracks of the South Shore Railroad. It was only a short trip to Chicago, probably the best liberty town in the country in those wartime years. All the Canteens, USOs, and similar organizations were highly visible and active, and free tickets, busy social schedules, land other resources were abundant.

On one of the busiest corners in downtown Chicago stands a huge, tall Methodist Church, and one Sunday two of us walked over in the warm summer morning to join the worshippers. After the service while participating in an informal social time, who should I encounter but Frank An-

137

drews, the Division Engineer from Whitehorse days. Typical of him, his first question was "How did you come out with the eye problem?"

"Good enough for the Navy," I replied, showing him the eye, now absent the patch in place at our last meeting in the hospital.

He had been temporarily assigned to Chicago, sent there to assist in preparing the final records of the Alaska Highway project, dubbed ALCAN by then. He proudly told me "We are finding the whole operation a credit to those involved. Other than a normally anticipated amount of confusion and the resultant inefficiencies, things prove to have been well executed. It should be a source of pride to all those involved. The whole cost is a little over $140 million".

It was a real encouragement to me to see a familiar face and be remembered as part of the Yukon team.

The Navy years passed quickly and without significant risk of life or limb, then it was back to Oregon State in the fall of 1946. In January, 1948 came the opportunity to take a qualifying test for a position as an engineering trainee for the Bureau of Public Roads, successor to the PRA. By qualifying I was appointed as one of six selected nationally to begin work during the summer break at the end of my sophomore year.

I found there many of the men with whom I had worked in the Yukon days, and was greeted particularly warmly by my old friend Archie Sawyer, even after five years. These earlier associations made easy the transition into the professional ranks at the end of 1950. At that time, with shiny new B.S. and B.A. degrees in Civil Engineering, I received a permanent appointment as a Highway Engineer, with duty to be in the Pacific Northwest. then Region 8.

After seven years as Resident Engineer on field projects and twelve years assigned to the Salem, Oregon Division office, In 11969, there came a transfer to Washington D.C. There I was first a member of the construction staff in the Federal Highway Projects division, later Chief of the Preliminary Engineering Branch.

It was while in this latter position that I was once again associated with the Alaska Highway.

On my birthday in 1973, the US congress enacted legislation providing for "Reconstruction of the Alaska Highway from the Alaskan border to Haines Junction in Canada and the Haines cutoff Highway from Haines Junction in Canada to the south Alaskan border". Accompanying this legislation was an authorization of $58,670,000 and the requirement that an agreement or treaty be reached between the two countries. the agreement was to include requirements for maintenance, free passage, reciprocal vehicle registration, and other pertinent items. All this was legislated without the knowledge, advice, or consent of the Canadian Government in Ottawa.

As one of very few in Washington who had any familiarity at all with the conditions and territory involved, I was selected as a member of the team to work out the international agreement.

First it was necessary to search the departmental archives and find the 1942 document under which the initial construction had been performed by the Army and PRA. Once found, fortunately it was possible to recycle the agreement to a great degree, thus simplifying the early stages of the negotiations.

With the thirty two year old agreement in hand, we were able to open discussions with our counterparts in Ottawa. It was time to tell them our Congress had decided to rebuild their road and we had come to talk about it.

Three trips were made to Ottawa, with discussions involving representatives from Region 8, Alaska, British Columbia, Public Works Canada, Canadian Bureau of Indian and Northern Affairs, and our Washington delegation.

By mid-1975 the issues had been resolved to the point where it was up to Congress and Parliament to approve the agreement so the project could move forward.

In early 1976 I was offered the opportunity to move to Vancouver, BC, and later, Whitehorse, to assume the duties as project manager for what had by then become the Shakwak Project, named after the broad valley it traversed.

After much thought and family discussion, I decided not to go back to the Yukon, but to retire after 31 years of service and return home to Oregon.

As a final contact with the highway, in 1975 came the opportunity to prepare the Alaska Highway portion of

139

AMERICAS HIGHWAYS, the bicentennial publication of the Federal Highway Administration. Despite the loss of most of the records through misunderstanding and accident, enough was still available to develop a creditable document.

Thus ended my official relationship with the Alaska Highway, but not my interest. Fortunately, in 1978 and again in 1985 I was able to make the trip north, and am planning more visits for the future.

Dedication Site

Appendix

CONSTRUCTION OF THE ALASKA HIGHWAY

Prepared for publication in
AMERICAS HIGHWAYS
Bicentennial Publication of the
FEDERAL HIGHWAY ADMINISTRATION
1975
Willis R. Grafe, Chief,
Preliminary Engineering Branch,
Federal Highway Projects Division,
Washington, D.C.

HISTORY OF CONSTRUCTION OF THE ALASKA HIGHWAY

The Decision

The Japanese attack on Pearl Harbor on December 7, 1941 and the subsequent Declaration of War by Germany and Italy involved the United States simultaneously in wars in both the Atlantic and Pacific areas.

This and closely following enemy successes in the Pacific found Alaska, on the great circle route between the U. S. and Japan, in a position highly exposed to attack. For the three or four weeks following the Pearl Harbor attack, virtually every merchant ship leaving west coast ports was attacked by enemy submarines.

On January 16, 1942, the President appointed a Cabinet Committee consisting of the Secretaries of Navy, War, and Interior to consider the necessity of a proper route for a highway to Alaska. On February 2, 1942, it was concluded that a highway was necessary and that it should fulfill two major requirements:

1. Furnish a supply route to link up the airfields established in 1941 in Canada and Alaska by the Canadian Government and Army Air Force.

2. Provide an auxiliary overland supply route to Alaska, relatively secure from attack by the enemy, to supplement sea and air routes and thus provide a measure of safety for the armed forces and aircraft ferrying personnel.

Prior to this action many studies had been made of the most desirable routing, but in the urgency for action, the military considerations were recognized to be of overriding importance.

The project was approved by the Army Chief of Staff on February 6, 1942; the President February 11, and work was authorized to begin at once. Final agreement with Canada was reached March 18, removing the last obstacle.

Termini for the work to be performed by U.S. forces were established Dawson Creek, B.C. and Big Delta, Alaska, where connections were to be made with existing transportation facilities.

The authorization provided for construction of a pioneer road by U.S. Army engineer troops who would be followed by contractors furnished and directed by the Public Roads Administration, (PRA) who would improve the pioneer road to an authorized standard.

In an exchange of letters March 4 and 16, the PRA received instructions from the War Department to build a final type of highway according to Specifications for Construction of Roads and Bridges in National Forests and Parks, 1941, designated as "FP 41" The road was to be two lanes with a subgrade wide enough for suitable surfacing which could be reduced to 20 or 22 feet if necessary. Surfacing was to be of local materials with final surfacing to be applied only after earthwork was stabilized. Temporary bridges were to be trestles of local timber. Permanent bridges were to be left to future financing and to the determination of the government authorities charged with operation of the road. The loading of temporary bridges was H-15. Trusses over 60 feet long and trestles over 100 feet long were to be 12 feet wide, otherwise, all bridge structures were to be 24 feet wide. Future steel bridges would be designed for H-20 loading. Initial culverts would be built of local timber, permanent culverts of poured concrete or pipe. Ruling grades would be a maximum 5 percent, maximum grade 7 percent; curvature on prairie routes would be 3 degrees, and in mountains 19 degrees, and all curves sharper than 3 degrees were to be spiralled. The sector commanders were to locate the pioneer road with such ultimate standards in mind in order to permit the final road to follow the pioneer route insofar as practicable.

As originally conceived, the work of constructing the highway was neatly divided between the engineer troops of the Army and civilian contractors under the direction of the PRA. In actuality, however, it was a combined effort with overlapping of work responsibility, shifts in emphasis, and a great deal of truly cooperative effort between the arrival of the first Army troops at Dawson Creek on Mar. 10, 1942, and the removal of all contractors personnel and supervisory engineers at the end of October, 1943.

As a highway project alone, ignoring military and economic considerations, the route selected was considered by many to be inferior to the one westerly of the main range of the Rocky Mountains, extending northward from Prince George, but there was a war going on, carrying with it a whole different set of priorities.

With the general route established there remained to be determined only the questions of canyons, rivers, mountain passes, muskeg, weather, native material sources, and other engineering and logistic considerations. The engineers were ready to take over from the policy makers.

MOBILIZATION

Immediately upon receiving notice of the impending agreement, Dr. L. I. Hewes, Chief, Western Headquarters, PRA, started a search of the whole West Coast of the U.S. for water transportation. A group of yachts, cargo vessels, tugs, and barges was finally assembled in Lake Union and Lake Washington in Seattle, and a management contractor, E.W. Elliott Co. of Seattle, was engaged to handle transportation and camp building. At the same time, Dr. Hewes also notified all personnel engaged in the PRA programs throughout the West that they were to make themselves available for duty on the Alaska Highway project. By virtue of over 20 years of roadbuilding on the Federal lands of the West, this group was already highly skilled and thoroughly familiar with the problems associated with highway engineering in rugged, primitive areas. These were the men who made PRA involvement in the Alaska highway a possibility and carried the work through to the crowning achievement which it ultimately became.

While all this was under way there was gathered up from the camps of the C.C.C. (Civilian Conservation Corps) in the Northwest, trucks, tools, and other equipment and materials for use on the project. These were started north by whatever transport could be obtained at their origin.

Following this, the resources of the WPA (Works Progress Administration) were tapped for roadbuilding and office equipment. Both these agencies were being terminated at the time, and utilization of surplus equipment was mutually beneficial.

Field headquarters were established in Whitehorse, Yukon Terr., and Ft. St. John, B.C., with subsidiary offices at

Ft. Nelson, on the Liard River 210 miles west of Ft. Nelson, Fairbanks, and Gulkana, Alaska.

PRA work in the Whitehorse sector was delayed more than one month behind that on the Ft. St. John end of the project. Whereas the first contingent of 12 from Denver led by Mr. Capes arrived in Ft. St. John on March 14 and 15, the first troops and PRA personnel reached Skagway early in April, with the Public Roads men reaching Whitehorse April 9-12. This group was headed by H. A. Stoddardt, J. B. Reher, and John McGillivray.

Access to the entire project was limited to three major routes as follows:

1. Via rail to Dawson Creek, B.C.
2. By boat to Skagway and rail to Whitehorse
3. By boat to Valdez and highway to Gulkana

This restricted access inevitably resulted in serious congestion at all the access points. Including Army shipments, 600 carloads arrived by rail at Dawson Creek within a period of 5 weeks in the spring of 1942. At one time 200 carloads were awaiting shipment at Prince Rupert, B.C., bound for Skagway or Valdez.

The level of activity soon made it apparent that a project Headquarters office needed to be established close to the scene of the action, and on April 20, 1942, J.S. Bright arrived in Seattle to establish a district office. This was moved to Edmonton in January, 1943.

RECONNAISSANCE AND LOCATION

Initial reconnaissance was conducted by air, on foot, and with pack trains and dog sleds. Other than aerial reconniassance, the Army Engineers were able to contribute little to establishment of the preliminary location of the highway in the southern sector.

Mr. C. F. Capes initiated the reconnaissance and location effort in the Ft. St. John sector, spending February 21-23 in company with Col. Wm. M. Hoge, Lt. Col. R. D. Ingalls, and escorted by Mr. H. P. Keith, Canadian Department of Transport on an automobile trip from Ft. St. John to Ft. Nelson and return over a winter road.

In mid-March ground reconnaissance along this same route was initiated by Eric Erhart and Alton O. Stinson, using the Canadian winter road as access. By virtue of being a winter road, this route was located through the wettest areas and on the frozen rivers, so the needs of an all-weather route required the new location to be some distance away. Establishment of the route on this 250 mile section from Ft. St. John to Ft. Nelson was almost solely through the efforts of these two men, transported only by their own two feet.

On Mar. 25, two reconnaissance parties set out to locate the most feasible line between the Sikanni Chief River and Watson Lake. From Ft. Nelson north to Watson Lake, W. H. Curwen and F. W. Ambos accompanied by two guides and two dog teams set out, and between that time and April 12 covered a total of over 330 miles. Simultaneously, J. L. Cheatham, O.P. Van Buskirk, W. H. Williams, and Paul E. Warren with guides formed two parties of five men and three sleds each and set out from the Sikanni Chief River for Ft. Nelson. They covered about 187 miles during the next 14 days. All this reconnaissance was performed in temperatures between minus 20F and +40F and with the exception of an occasional trapper's cabin they lived in the open under a canvas fly.

The route in this area was the subject of much controversy and on April 23, Mr. Capes again flew aerial reconnaissance with General Hoge. This continued intermittently through the 26th, with continuing pressure on Mr. Capes to reach a decision so the troops at Ft. Nelson could begin work. On April 26, despite failure to completely agree with the Army, Mr. Capes made his written recommendations so they could proceed.

Thus the Army was given a sense of direction, and started into the bush. Despite all the location activity, however, significant construction did not start on the southern end of the route until well into June. Both weather and lack of transport were continually uncooperative.

Sixty pack horse outfits were organized at the beginning of May to accompany survey crews working out of Ft. Nelson, and Public Roads engineers began flagging line for the Army clearing crew. Army and Public Roads location parties moved north together from Ft. St. John to establish the truck trail location in late May.

Aerial reconnaissance was the principal guide in locat-

149

ing the route from Watson Lake to Whitehorse, and the best crossing over the divide between the Mckenzie and Yukon river systems on this sector was pointed out by Les Cook, a bush flyer. The summit was only 3208 feet, substantially lower than indicated on published. maps.

Fortunately, the Army Air Corps had, during the fall of 1941 photographed much of the area between the airfields in Canada and was further able, in the spring and summer of 1942 to do more complete photography along many of the possible routes observed from aerial reconnaissance or the initial photographs. These new photographs were quickly made available to the location engineers in the field camps, enabling them by use of compass and prominent landmarks to locate critical "control" points in the route selection. Much of the time, particularly in the Ft. St. John sector, this line was flagged and blazed by the locator for the bulldozer operators on the pioneer road. Construction was sometimes done so closely behind the locators that at times they expressed fear of being run over in the process.

This use of aerial photographs was a new technique for the times, and as the season progressed and confidence mounted, more and more competence was acquired, making this phase of the project a true proving ground for highway location by aerial survey methods.

East and west of Whitehorse, while the aerial reconnaissance was still under way in April, ground survey crews were flown in, landing on yet frozen lakes, and location surveys started along the lines previously flown. Later, aerial photographs of the route location corridor were made available to the survey crews. Some of these crews, transported by boat or pack string, did not have outside contact except for resupply by the same methods or float plane until into September. In some areas ground reconnaissance was not really completed until after location surveys had started, but no significant rerunning of surveys resulted from such scheduling.

Ground reconnaissance was started May 10 in the area from Burwash Landing on the Northwesterly end of Kluane Lake west to the junction of the Nebesna and Chesana rivers. Already about ten miles of survey had been done from Burwash Landing to beyond the Duke river, where control points were easily identified. This long section of over 300 miles was performed by John McGillivray of PRA accompanied by Major W.W. Hodge, Capt. S.C. Baker, Pfc. Kenneth Dillinger, two native Indian guides and 21 head of pack and saddle horses. These men passed the location survey crews which were already at work on portions of the route, and were guided by maps, trails, and the knowledge of the native guides.

Thus was the original location performed, and the surveys guided to an integrated effort during the summer of 1942. The permanent surveys were completed in December with the final gaps closed near Watson Lake by crews brought down from the western Yukon after they had completed their originally assigned sections near the Alaska border.

In early spring, 1942, as soon as field notes began to come in to Dawson Creek, a Design Office under Mr. Wm. T. Pryor was established and constuction plans to the agreed standards were prepared. This office was later moved to Ft. St. John after PRA contractors started work on the last week of May.

Most of the final design plans were prepared during the winter in anticipation of contract construction of the completed road in 1943.

CONSTRUCTION, 1942

The rate of actual construction in 1942 is difficult to conceive, but the fact that practically all the pioneer road was built in five months and most of it in four gives an idea of the speed which was necessary. The Army involvement in construction consisted of seven engineer regiments who proceeded as follows:

The 35th Engineers arrived at Dawson Creek March 10, 1942, and had transported all its equipment to Ft. Nelson over the winter road by April 15. Spring rain delayed the work and little was accomplished until mid-June. With the assistance of the 341st, they cleared the route to Contact Creek, south of Watson Lake and a linkup with the 340th.

The 341st Engineers arrived in Dawson Creek in April, but equipment did not arrive until June. Their clearing parties beginning at Ft. St. John, reached Ft. Nelson August 24th, then assisted the 35th and also doubled back to improve their portion to a better standard.

The 95th Engineers arrived at Dawson Creek in June and followed up the 341st clearing operations. The work performed by these regiments was almost completely restricted to a tote trail, usable by all-terrain vehicles, and conversion to a usable road was performed primarily by civilian contractors.

The 18th Engineers arrived in Skagway in mid-April and Whitehorse

151

by May 1. This regiment improved the road west from the Tahkini River to Kluane Lake and did the pioneer construction from there to Beaver Creek near the International boundary, where it met the 97th on October 25.

The 340th Engineers arrived in Skagway April 21, waiting there until June for equipment, then moved to Whitehorse. There they were divided, part working west from Whitehorse and the remainder, after being shipped to Teslin by boat, worked east and west from there. Their east group met the 35th at Contact Creek on Sept. 24.

The 93rd Engineers arrived at Skagway April 20 and waited until June for equipment. They then were moved to Carcross and worked east to Teslin Lake.

The 97th Engineers arrived at Valdez, Alaska, April 3, spent six weeks working on the Gulkana road, then on July 1 jumped to Slana and worked north, arriving at Tanacross August 25. From Tanacross in cooperation with contractors Lytle and Green, they moved eastward to meet the 18th Engineers October 25 at Beaver Creek, closing the final gap in the pioneer road.

Immediately upon start of construction by the Army troops came the realization that without help from the Public Roads Contractors, it would not be possible to complete the access road or keep anything resembling the originally planned schedule, and the work forces began to be merged. This began with requests by Brigadier General Wm. M. Hoge, Army Officer in Charge, to assist in ballasting, general assistance to engineer regiments, and for contractors to build entire sections of the road. This participation by the contractors expanded on an informal basis as well, until in some areas construction became almost totally a partnership affair. By the end of July contractors were being shifted about and reorganized all up and down the line to supplement and speed up construction of the pioneer road without regard to prior arrangements or schedules.

Finally, Maj. Gen. C. L. Sturdevant, Assistant Chief of Engineers, after a conference with Public Roads Engineers and Sector Commanders, decided to discard the original formula of separate forces and concentrated the combined effort on construction of the pioneer road in 1942. All civilian forces were instructed to support the Army, both Engineers and Contractors.

Progress improved drastically as a result of the implementation of this decision, and it soon became evident some hope might still be entertained for completion of the truck trail before freeze-up.

Army requests for the construction of the Dawson Creek railhead, pipeline, flight strips, and other installations, cou-

pled with a labor shortage and increasing equipment breakdowns and parts shortages compounded to further delay the
work despite the closest kind of cooperation. Perseverance
prevailed, however, and on October 25 the final breakthrough
came at Beaver Creek in the Yukon, near the Alaska border.
A formal ceremony at Soldiers Summit, on the south end
of Kluane Lake, celebrated the event on November 20, 1942.

WINTER, 1942

Subsequent to the breakthrough, much remained to be
done to make the truck trail a usable road. The westerly portion presented a dreary prospect, and work continued on
into the winter under extreme weather conditions. Sometimes temperatures reached 50 to 60 degrees below zero.
Diesel fuel failed to flow from the fuel tanks to the engines,
and steel parts broke with increasing frequency. The temporary bridges were freezing in or going out when newly
formed ice pulled them apart. Winterizing of camps was being rushed.

In early December the Army announced it would assume
responsibility for all winter maintenance, only to change its
mind in mid-January and throw it all back onto the civilian
forces. All through the winter work continued at a fairly high
level on major structures on the Peace, Sikanni Chief, Musk-
wa, and Liard rivers, and on rock excavation where possible. Preparation was made for the 1943 season by repair of
equipment and construction of shops and camps. Record low
temperatures were encountered, reaching 70 below in Whitehorse and 72 below on the northern sector.

Engineering work in preparation for the following year
was carried on continually throughout the winter, both in
the U.S. and in project offices, and the design for the permanent highway was completed by the beginning of the 1943
season. Just as the designs were being finalized, on April
7, 1943, the Army issued a directive drastically reducing the
standards and requiring following of the route of the truck
trail to the maximum extent feasible for a usable road.

In retrospect, the first year was one of many problems
of logistics, establishment, and reestablishment of policy, in-
consistencies, conflict, and, finally, on-the-ground cooperation by the job personnel, regardless of status. A truck trail

153

of sorts was built, much of it improved to a usable, all weather standard, and the construction of a highway in 1943 made a possibility. Despite all the unanticipated, ever changing, and conflicting requests from the Army, the PRA and its contractors had been able to mobilize and equip to perform the originally assigned task for 1943.

CONSTRUCTION, 1943

The road as it had evolved by the end of 1943 was constructed almost entirely in that year, but the original road resulting from the 1942 effort must be given full credit for its contribution of communication and transport to the final effort.

The April 7 directive, mentioned earlier, caused a drastic shift in emphasis for the 1943 efforts of the contractors under the direction of the PRA. As a result, the final road contained a substantial mileage of out-of-direction location, excessively steep grades, and dangerous alignment. This was an outgrowth of the fact that the original road had been constructed to a large degree along the lines of least resistance. No appreciable resources had been available at the time for locating a permanent, all weather, and reasonably safe facility.

The spring breakup during May destroyed a large number of the temporary bridges south of Watson Lake, but stockpiled materials enabled rapid replacement for the season. This was a temporary setback, but progress was maintained by a work force of over 11,000 men. Weather throughout June seriously delayed the anticipated schedule on the southerly section, and further washouts of structures again delayed the work. Despite this, work on the major structures was not seriously impeded and some were put into use in the late spring. The number of men remained constant throughout most of the season, with some reduction of bridge workload as structures were completed compensated for in expansion of the grading effort.

The severe bottleneck in fuel supply at the Peace River Ferry was relieved by hanging a two inch line from the suspension cables, coupled with use of storage tanks on the north side of the river.

By mid-June the northern portion had thawed and

warmed enough for work to start on most operations and the major structures were near schedule.

Disaster struck heavily on July 9 and 10 when 200 miles on each side of Ft. Nelson a heavy rain caused the destruction of 124 temporary bridges. A coordinated effort by all forces, utilizing, once more, stockpiled and salvaged materials, resulted in reopening for through traffic by July 20, nearly two weeks sooner than the most optimistic estimates.

Despite these setbacks, good progress was made, and in July the Ft. St. John sector was opening new sections of road and new bridges almost daily. The opening of the Peace River Bridge to one-way traffic August 4 and later that month to two-way traffic, was a significant relief, despite the temporary loss of six more bridges to high water west of Ft. Nelson early in August. Fortunately, by this time it had become almost routine to replace such spans, and five days later traffic was once again on the move.

The Army continued to issue a virtual snowstorm of instructions and directives, withdrawing previous approvals of permanent structures and routings of the highway. Finally the type of final surfacing was downgraded to selected borrow rather than crushed rock. Contractors were also required to construct airstrips and perform grading for the telephone relay stations and maintenance stations. All a legitimate part of fighting a war, but disconcerting, nevertheless.

As late as mid-August the 40 mile section near the Alaska-Yukon border which had been constructed after the 1942 freezeup was still impassable. No access to the area was possible except by float planes, which were used to ferry men and supplies for camp construction. Contractors from both north and south continued their efforts in the area, using "swamp cats" with extra width treads field fabricated from salvaged parts. Finally on October 13 the gap was closed, permanently reopening the road. Over the next two weeks it was improved to an acceptable standard through a concentrated effort by all.

On October 6 the Army decided that all work would be completed by October 31, so schedules were developed for evacuation and the southward migration of men and equipment began. Neither grading nor surfacing was complete on the deadline date, but in accordance with Army instructions, all work stopped, leaving the rest to maintenance forces.

By October 31, ninety-nine bridges had been completed and 34 were either under construction or not yet started. The latter were at locations where Army approval had not been received until August or September and steel delivery was impossible in 1943.

It was contemplated that the permanent bridges would be completed in 1944 under Public Roads supervision with a design office in Edmonton and a construction engineer in Whitehorse. All designs were completed, and the required structural steel had been fabricated and shipped to Whitehorse during the winter of 1943-44. Subsequently all permanent bridges in Canada with the exception of the Teslin river were eliminated, and work was completed on it under an Army contract October 5, 1944. The complete story of the bridge program is an epic in itself which space does not afford telling.

The construction performed in 1943 completed with a gravel surface all sections of the highway located and designed by the PRA where grading had been well started at the time of the April 7 directive. Work on which clearing but no significant grading had been completed was at that time abandoned, and the contractors were assigned to improvement of the pioneer road to a usable condition This was the picture the highway presented at the end of October when the initial construction forces were withdrawn.

PEOPLE AND EQUIPMENT

At the peak of operations in September, 1943, there were 1,850 PRA employes and 14,100 civilian employees of 181 contractors working with 11,107 units of equipment, of which 3,983 were contractor owned and 7,124 government owned. The latter were primarily from CCC, WPA, and Army sources. As with the pioneer road, the 1420 miles of final highway was largely built in a four month period, and at a total final cost of $130,595,000.

Transportation to and from the project, both freight and personnel, was handled by Contractor E. W. Elliott of Seattle. The fleet consisted of four freighters, ten tugboats, 5 passenger boats (converted yachts), and one manned barge, built

156

in 1868. In addition, early contingents of personnel were carried to Skagway by the Army Transportation Service, either classified as passengers or cargo, depending on order of boarding and location of berth above or below decks. The total quantities handled in the construction of the final road by the PRA and its contractors added up to 22,953,000 cu.yds. of earthwork, 133 bridges over 20 feet long, for a total of seven miles, over 8000 culverts for a total of over 52 miles, and 7,153,000 cubic yards of ballast and surfacing. Suspension bridges over the Peace River (2130') and Lower Liard (989') were the most notable structures, but several other major treated timber and steel trusses were constructed during the winter and spring of 1942-43 and through the subsequent season.

Once estasblished, the PRA organization was relatively stable for the full life of the project, staffed almost exclusively with engineering and support personnel from the Western United States.

The headquarters office of the Alaska Highway District was initially established in Seattle, but subsequently moved to Edmonton, Alberta on January 15, 1943. Field operations were directed through two Division offices, located at Ft. St. John, B.C. and Whitehorse, Yukon Teritory. A sub-office of Ft. St. John was established at Ft. Nelson and a similar one at Tok Junction, Alaska, under the Whitehorse Division.

The District office was headed by J. S. Bright, assisted by N.F. McCoy as Associate District Engineer. L.M. Huggins and George M. Williams were in charge of Engineering and Operations. Raymond A. Archibald was in charge of the Bridge program, Frank R. Carlen was office Engineer, property and equipment was under Forrest R. Hall, and Francis C. turner supervised the warehousing operation.

The Ft. St. John Division, which supervised the 567 miles from Dawson Creek to just south of Watson Lake was originally headed by Levant Brown, who was suceeded by C.F. Capes. Locating engineers were Eric E. Erhart and Carl Schubert, and Field Construction Operations were directed by Fred J. Dixon, W.J. Nelson, and T.M. Roach. W.T. Pryor was Administrative Engineer for Design, Statistical Data, and Reports. J.C. Williams was responsible for Public Health, Relations with the management Contractors, and Procurement.

157

R.R. Tipton was Bridge Engineer and W.T. Thornblad was Equipment Supervisor.

The Whitehorse Division, including the office at Tok Junction, was responsible for the portion from a point just south of Watson Lake to the junction with the Richardson Highway, a distance of 853 miles.

Frank E. Andrews was Division Enginer, assisted by C.G. Polk at Tok and Hugh A. Stoddardt in Canada. Bridge Engineer was J.B. Robertson, J.B. Reher was Chief Locating Engineer, L.A. DeKlotz was Materials Engineer, and John MacGillivray, D.H. Cadmus, E.N. Moore, and J.H. Brannan were field supervisors. Harry S. Tolen was in charge of the Utah Construction Company Field Operations, a separate contract from the other management contractors. At Tok, Polk was assisted by W.R. Bringolf on bridges, F. LeRoy Davis, H.L. Oakley and E.L. Jordan as Supervisors, and W.L. Eager as Materials Engineer.

Much more could be said about such things as physical camp facilities, transportation, procurement, medical services and sanitation, and the multitude of other factors which entered into the completion of the project. The inability to cover them all in detail here is not through a lack of respect for and recognition of their value to the completed project, but through lack of space. The many human interest stories of hardship, privation, isolation, and sheer grit and courage in the face of adversity could fill volumes, and their ultimate loss to posterity for failure of a written record can only be deplored.

During the winter of 1943-44 an extensive study was made of icing conditions on the highway. Data so acquired contributed to the development of methods to alleviate many of the problems caused by failure to build into the road proper safeguards for winter travel and maintenance.

WHO WERE THE PRA ENGINEERS?

Location, design and construction of the military road to Alaska was a job tailor made for the skills of the Public Roads Adminstration.

Since 1905 their predecessors had been involved in work on the Federal domain. Since 1907 when the National Forests were created, a road office had been in existence in the Department of Agriculture.

In 1914 a Division of National Park and Forest Roads was established in the Agriculture Department, charged with the responsiblity to coordinate roadbuilding in the Departments of Agriculture and Interior, managers of the Federal lands.

The magnitude of the need can be understood to a degree by the realization that in 1918 there were 274,000 square miles of National Forests alone. By 1940 it had increased to over 300,000 square miles, larger than the combined areas of the states of California, Oregon, and a fourth of Washington. By 1940, prior to the beginning of World War II there were more than 140 National Park areas as well, many in remote areas, and in the west almost completely surrounded by National Forests.

Virtually all the National Forests are on the slopes of the Rocky, Cascade, or Sierra Nevada mountains, ranges forming north-south barriers to transportation across the country from Mexico to Canada. As late as 1920 there were still no year round east-west roads across the ranges in Oregon or Washington. The very recently completed road in the Columbia River Gorge was the only access from the western slope to the inland empire, and in winter it was at times impassable.

This lack of a basic transportation network and the great distances involved led to the establishment, in 1921, of a Western Headquarters by the then Bureau of Public roads in San Francisco. Six western Districts were located at Portland, San Francisco, Denver, Missoula, Ogden, and Albuquerque, sites already containing Forest Service regional headquarters.

All through the 1920s and 1930s, a relatively high level

159

of work continued in developing access to the isolated Federal lands of the west, with breakthroughs made on many cross mountain routes. Once the conections were made, they were turned over to the States for ownership and maintenance.

In the National Parks as well, a high level of activity was in progress, opening up the wonders of the west for the enjoyment of the rest of the country. One look at the construction as evidenced in the Zion-Mt.Carmel Tunnel, Trail Ridge Road in Rocky Mountain Park, or the roads in Yosemite and Rainier Parks is enough to convince even the most skeptical that the PRA was surely an engineering organization competent to take on virtually any roadbuilding challenge outdoors.

During the depths of the depression of the 1930's additional funding was provided as a means of creating employment. It was during those years that the Bureau of Public Roads was moved from within the Dept. of Agriculture to the newly created Federal Works agency and the name changed to Public Roads Administration.

Those were the years of preparation for the work in 1942 and 1943 in British Columbia, Yukon, and Alaska.

There the days and years, in remote and rugged areas, living in tent camps at the mercy of the pack horses, mosquitoes, and severe weather, were to pay off in an understanding and acceptance of the work to be done. Here was acquired the capability to move ahead with confidence when called on.

The north country wasn't anywhere near as rugged as that of the mountains where the passes go up to ten thousand feet and one or more tunnels may be necessary on most of the routes across the mountains, but the problems of muskeg, permafrost, longer-lived mosquitoes and colder and longer winters required learning a lot of new things.

The open ended wartime contracts caused much anguish to field engineers accustomed to the tightly controlled work of the depression years. Isolation forced Project Engineers to make decisions and improvise, all the while agonizing over how U.S. dollars were being used more loosely than they had ever experienced.

All told, it must be said the PRA personnel from top to

bottom were well prepared for the task assigned. The job
was not so much an engineering challenge as one of logistics, flexibility, and disruption of their personal life, the latter of which, in wartime, soon came to be accepted, albeit
not without a bit of grumbling.

CREW ROSTERS

Roster of survey party led by Fred Johnson, performing
seventy miles of preliminary location survey from east of Burwash Landing to the White River, 1942 May-September

Fred M. Johnson	Chief of Party
Lowell Jensen	Draftsman and Asst. Chief
M.W. (Bill) Ash	Transitman
J.H. (Tuck) Tucker	Levelman
Cecil L. Lacy	Topographer
Harry Z. French	Head Chainman
Ken Strawn	Computer and map maker
Archie C. Erickson	Rodman-chainman
Clyde Hill	Rodman-chainman
Hugh E. Kelly	Rodman-chainman
Billie W. Bassett	Rodman-chainman
Jack Edwards	Rodman-chainman
Willis Grafe	Rodman-chainman
Louis Montalva, Jr.	Rodman-chainman
Tom Kirkwood	Bushman
Louis Vuckovich	Short time Axeman
Ray Hinton	Cook
Jimmie Joe	Packer
Sam Johnson	Packer
Louis Jacquot	Wrangler

Roster of survey party led by Roy Lednicky, performing
twenty miles of traverse and topog of Army road in British
Columbia just south of Lower Post on the Liard River. Temperatures to -40F.

Roy Lednicky	Chief of Party
Chuck Ellis	Draftsman and office man
Don Reid	Transitman
Doug White	Levelman
Walter Green	Head Chainman

Emery Waller	Topographer
Archie Erickson	Rodman-Chainman
Peter Herschenberger	Rodman-Chainman
Peter Heisel	Rodman-Chainman
Louis Montalva	Rodman-Chainman
Hugh E. Kelly	Rodman-Chainman
Phillip Englebrecht	Rodman-Chainman
Hugh P. Taylor	Rodman-Chainman
Willis Grafe	Rodman-Chainman
Andy Isaacson	Cook
Gordon Ray	Flunky

Roster of John Haapala's party, performing twelve miles of construction survey from Haines north up the Chilkat River, November, 1942-April 1943. Relieved to go back to the interior by U.S. Enginering Dept. (USED) and Foley Construction Co.

J. E. Haapala	Chief of Party
Donald Reid	Transitman
Doug White	Levelman
Emery Waller	Levelman
Jack Obermeyer	Head Chainman
Richard S. Pozzi	Rear Chain
Roy Canfield	Rodman-Chainman
Don Gedney	Rodman-Chainman
Hector Langdon	Rodman-Chainman
Willis Grafe	

Roster of Construction survey and engineering crew supervised by Archie Sawyer. Forty miles of construction of Alaska highway from Summit Creek,(Mile 121) west to beyond Soldiers Summit and completion of ten miles of work from Donjek River northwest. Elliott Construction Co, Contractor. Completed Nov. 1, 1943.

Arch Sawyer,	Chief of Party and Resident Engineer
Bill Hebert	Transitman
Clem Davis	Transitman
Mel Hewett	Transitman
Misisippi Taylor	Rodman Chainman
Spud Canfield	Levelman

162

Claude Swentkofske	Rodman Chainman
Ed J. Jankowski	Transitman
Al Garrissere	Office Man
Myron Thompson	Bridge Engineer
John C. Anderson	Rodman Chainman
Jim Holderman	Levelman
Bruce Farnham	Canadian Student
A.W.S. Tite	Canadian Student
Les Nelson	Canadian Student
Anatol Roshko	Canadian Student
Tony Madsen	Rodman Chainman
Chet Kaiser	Rodman Chainman
Sammy McCaw	Canadian Student
Miller	Canadian Student
Gerhard Oien	Rodman Chainman
Jack Obermeyer	Levelman
Stan Brown	Transitman
H. Slattery	Unsuccessful Asst. Chief
Junior Carpenter	Rodman Chainman
Willis Grafe	Levelman and Rodman Chainman

Sources

The Alaska Highway, First Year, Theodore A. Huntley, Senior Administrative Officer, Federal Works Agency, Assigned to the Public Roads Administration, Edmonton, Alberta, Canada, March 31, 1943.

Construction of the Alaska Highway, First year, 1942 Condensation of Report by Theodore A. Huntley, Senior Administrative Officer.

Second Year, 1943 Report by R. E. Royall, Senior Highway Engineer, Washington, D.C. September 1945.

Supplement to the Huntley-Royall Report on Construction of the Ft. St. John Division of the Alaska Highway C. F. Capes, Denver, Colo. June, 1944.

The Alaska Highway, An Interim Report from the Committee on Roads House of Representatives, Pursuant to H. Res. 255, Authorizing the Committee on Roads as a whole or by subcommittees to investigate the Federal Road system and for other Purposes. March 13, 1946. USGPO

Alcan, Americas Glory Road An Engineering News Record report in three parts by Harold W. Richardson.

Part I Strategy and Location, December 17, 1942, pp 83-96

Part II Supply, Equipment and Camps, Dec. 31, 1942 pp 35-42

Part III Construction Tactics, January 14, 1943, pp 131-138

Canada-Alaska highway Reconnaissance report, Northway Airfield — Snag and Beaver Creeks F. LeRoy Davis, June, 1942.

Canada-Alaska Highway Reconnaissance report, Burwash Landing — Tanana River John McGillivray, June, 1942.

Aerial Reconnaissance Report, Ft. Nelson to Watson Lake section C. F. Capes, April 29, 1942.

Report of Dog Team Reconnaissance Trips, Ft. Nelson to Watson Lake and Sikanni Chief River to Ft. Nelson, March 25 to April 12, 1942, W. H. Curwen and W. H. Willesen, No date.

Aerial Surveying on the Alaska Highway, 1942 William T. Pryor, Public Roads Magazine Vol. 24, No. 11, January-February, March, 1947.

Ice Formation on the Alaska Highway William L. Eager and William T. Pryor Public Roads Magazine, Vol. 24, No. 3, January, February, March, 1945.